Praise for
Coach Your Se.

As the CEO of your own destiny, leveraging your strengths is not enough—
you also need to know where you may be holding yourself back. Mike
Normant's *Coach Your Self Up* helps you not only see where you are imposing
limits on yourself, it teaches you the steps to make sustainable positive
changes.

—Maynard Webb, Founder of Webb Investment Network, Co-Founder of
Everwise, Bestselling Author of Rebooting Work, Board Member at Visa &
Salesforce

"This book is a "must-add" to your personal and career development library.
How we behave and the way we interact with others has a big impact on our
career and life opportunities. Mike Normant's *Coach Your Self Up* pushes you
to look in the mirror and honestly assess where you may be unknowingly
blocking your own success. Building on a superb overview and synopsis of
the work of important thought leaders in the fields of psychology and human
behavior, Mike shares a step-by-step process for making small shifts that can
lead to big changes for you."

—Dr. Beverly Kaye, Founder of Career Systems International, Speaker, Co-
Author of *Help Them Grow or Watch Them Go, Up is Not the Only Way, Love 'Em
or Lose 'Em*

"The worlds of personal and career development are merging. Focusing on
personal growth at work is part of bringing our whole selves to work. The best
thing we can do to move forward in our careers is to make a commitment to
our own personal development—to deepening our self-awareness. Mike
Normant's *Coach Your Self Up* provides a powerful self-coaching toolkit that
enables this growth."

—Mike Robbins, Author of *Bring Your Whole Self to Work*

"Mike Normant nails it with his premise that personal development *is* career
development. Any work you can do with yourself to shift self-limiting
patterns will absolutely benefit you on the job. *Coach Your Self Up* provides
you with a pragmatic framework and tools to help you identify your own self-
limiting patterns and to self-coach your way to making lasting changes.

—Stuart Crabb, Partner and Founder, Oxegen Consulting, former Global
Head of Learning at Facebook

"Mike Normant's *Coach Your Self Up* touches two fundamental beliefs we share at 1440—it all begins with self-awareness, and the answers we seek are found only within each of us, for ourselves. Self-coaching follows naturally, helping everyone to guide their own career journeys to the growth and understanding that will take them to the next level."

—**Scott Kriens,** Co-Founder, 1440 Multiversity

"Bookstore shelves are filled with books telling readers what kind of person to be in order to be happy, successful, stress-free and so on. But many of them miss the point entirely—the hard part for people isn't figuring out what they could be, but how to get there. It's difficult to bring one's best self forward— yet to be successful in our work and in our lives, that's the help we really need. Mike's *Coach Your Self Up* provides a roadmap for exactly that."

—**Todd Murtha**, CEO, Careerwave

"*Coach Your Self Up* is a gift directly out of the depths of Mike's life itself, reflecting an accumulation of learnings from his professional experiences along with years of his ongoing pursuit of his best self. This book is as powerful as it is practical and approachable, providing tools, guidance and inspiration to make consequential changes in your career, work and life!"

—**Michael Lipson,** CEO Whisperer, Executive Coach, Culture Builder & Strategist

"I'm in full agreement with Mike Normant's belief that rising levels of self-awareness has the potential for profound effects in the world. Seeing one's self more clearly leads to new habits and behaviors. *Coach Your Self Up* will not only help you be more successful in your career, it can also positively impact the individuals, teams, and organizations that you are part of."

—**Aaron Kahlow**, Founder of ConsciousLeader.org and Founder/Chief Facilitator of Conscious Circles

"Our habitual thought patterns get in the way of being our best selves. In my work I see this every day. The world needs more pragmatic tools to help people "wake up" to their inner potential. Mike Normant's Coach Your Self Up is one of those tools. This highly accessible book is meant not only to be read, but to be applied."

—**Segyu Choepel Rinpoche,** Master and Holder of the Segyu Tibetan Buddhist Lineage, Founder and Director of Juniper Integrative Care Clinic

"Benjamin Franklin once said, "There are three things extremely hard, steel, a diamond, and to know one's self." Lucky for us, Mike Normant's new book *Coach Your Self Up* has made it easier for us to accomplish this. Using clear language, concise concepts representing current research and transformational practices that are creative and experience based, he guides readers through a self-learning process that leads the student into more expanded self-awareness. Always compassionate in his view of the difficulties along the way, he keeps us present, engaged and on point as we learn about our self from our self. I highly recommend it!"

—**Gary Sherman**, Founder of the Creative Awareness Project and Author of *Perceptual Integration: The Mechanics of Awakening*

"Creating a "conscious culture" is the cornerstone of the Conscious Capitalism four-tenets framework. The self-coaching skills introduced in Coach Your Self Up are specifically designed to serve in activating individuals to become more aware of, and responsible for their human-ness, in other words, becoming more conscious. I believe that organizations that aspire to develop and sustain a conscious culture should definitely consider Coach Your Self Up as a high-impact component of any personal development and performance initiatives in amplifying the amazing potential of their employees. Mike's thoughtful and practical approach in this book is a huge contribution to the movement toward humanity-centered business."

—**Steve Havill**, Founder and CEO of Conscia Ventures, Board President of Conscious Capitalism Bay Area Chapter

The Unlimit Group Publishing
San Francisco, CA 94102

The **Unlimit** Group
Remove limits. Bend your future.

URL for the eLearning program: coachyourselfup.com/course/paperback

Library of Congress Cataloging-in-Publication Data
LCN Number: 2018905921

ISBN: 978-1-7321931-0-9

Editors: Alice Chaffee and Linda Newlin

Cover and Interior Image Design: Ina Murdock-Santos, The Branding Room
Initial Logo Design: Chelsea Rae Cole, Design & Photo

Dedicated to the thought leaders and teachers, past and present, whose work helps individuals unleash their full potential.

Contents

Preface

Hello, and welcome to Coach Your Self Up®. I am thrilled that you are exploring this new frontier of coaching to support your ongoing personal and career development. The techniques and practices presented in this book are for individuals who are seeking to make positive shifts in their careers and their lives.

About You

You are interested in taking more ownership of your career, seeking to better understand and proactively utilize the career levers that are in your control.

You believe, or are open to the idea, that the best thing you can do to drive your career success is to commit to your ongoing personal growth, to working with/on yourself.

You realize that shifts you make through personal development at work will spill over into all aspects of your life.

You are interested in working on yourself to be more effective, to be a better version of yourself, and to tap into more and more of your full potential.

You are interested in learning a pragmatic approach to making sustainable behavior changes, an approach that you can use over and over again throughout your life.

You appreciate the importance of "being present" and are seeking tools that can help you improve in this regard.

You recognize, or are open to the possibility, that sometimes you get in your own way.

You are aware of, or open to finding out about, specific behaviors you engage in that are counterproductive to your success.

You are aware, or open to learning, that you are wired to create stories (i.e., assumptions, conclusions, opinions, beliefs) about your world and about yourself. These stories can also be self-limiting.

You are interested in learning to cultivate a self-observation practice to deepen your self-awareness.

I hope you find this book to be a valuable resource in your professional and personal development journey.

About Me

I would love to share the story of how Coach Your Self Up® came into being.

In 2007, while running the global Learning and Development department of a pre-IPO tech company based in San Francisco, I went through a divorce. Although the divorce was collaborative and generally amicable, it was a stressful and draining experience.

In early 2008, the ink was barely dry on the divorce papers and my ex-wife ended up in the hospital for an extended period of time facing a serious health crisis, from which, thankfully, she emerged. Shortly thereafter, I lost my beloved mother.

People from all facets of my life were there for me and delivered a consistent message of, "You need to take a break and take care of yourself." I finally listened and left my job (on good terms!) in the summer of 2011. My intent was to take four to six months off to recharge my batteries and then go "do it again" (i.e., run the Learning and Development function at a locally-based company).

Then the universe intervened. Friends recommended books. I read some Eckhart Tolle, some Deepak Chopra, some Wayne Dyer and more. Many of these personal growth philosophies and ideas resonated with me.

Preface

I spent almost a year and a half attending numerous meetings and events with a men's "consciousness group" that a friend had recommended. It was fantastic. I learned so many things about how to "work with/on myself" from that group.

During this time, three different friends mentioned to me a weekend program called LifeLaunch® led by The Hudson Institute of Coaching in Santa Barbara, CA. The weekend was designed to help people reflect on their lives and to create a vision and a plan for a meaningful path forward.

When LifeLaunch® was mentioned to me for the third time, I decided that the universe wanted me to go and I signed up for the next program in the fall of 2011.

A few important things happened during that LifeLaunch® weekend: I gave myself permission to take an entire year off to process the recent upheaval in my life and I decided to enroll in Hudson's eight-month program to become a certified coach.

One important aspect of Hudson's Coach-in-Training (CIT) program was called "Self-as-Coach" and was all about becoming more self-aware. So, there I was, working with a men's consciousness group in parallel with Hudson's CIT program. It was self-awareness development on steroids.

In the summer of 2012, I decided to try and make it on my own. I would lead management and leadership training programs inside fast-growing tech companies.

Along the way, I continued to tell people about some of the personal breakthroughs I'd experienced on the self-awareness front and how that was leading to some life-changing shifts.

During 2013 and 2014, more people started saying things like "Mike, it seems like this self-awareness stuff has been pretty transformative for you, why don't you build a training program to share it with others?" In the summer of 2014 I put my head down and set out to do just that.

My intention was to create a program that could be delivered to cohorts within organizations. And I wanted to make it relevant to any interested employee, regardless of level or role.

I know that many organizations invest in leadership development programs for their managers and senior leaders. Raising self-awareness is typically a key aspect of these programs. I wanted to bring this aspect of leadership development to a broader audience. Why not bring the gifts and benefits of increased self-awareness to all employees?

With the support and guidance and coaching of lots of good people, a solid program design began to emerge. I got more and more excited about this and eventually came up with a name for the program: "Coach Your Self Up." I soon found two companies that were excited to run a pilot of the classroom training program for a cohort of interested employees. The results were promising.

Fast forward to 2017. Whenever I shared my purpose with others (to raise self-awareness in the world to help as many people as possible achieve more of their potential), they would tell me, "You need to write a book." I resisted this for several months.

It finally became clear to me that not only could I write this book, but that at some level my purpose demanded it. I had created something powerful that was already benefiting people in the classroom. If my intention was to impact as many lives as possible, I needed to make this material available to individuals.

> As I reflect on my journey of these last several years, I see that I have been applying the Coach Your Self Up self-coaching principles and skills all along the way.

The beauty of Coach Your Self Up® is that it takes relatively complex topics and makes them accessible and easy to understand. I hope you find this to be true for you.

As I write this in early 2018, the Coach Your Self Up® classroom training program has been delivered at multiple companies, including the first international delivery in Chennai, India. Participant feedback has been very strong. It feels fantastic to hear anecdotes from folks who have been able to apply principles from Coach Your Self Up® to make positive shifts in their own lives.

> *Here are two brief excerpts from the testimonials in Appendix A:*
>
> "This program was nothing short of transformative for me. It's been great to see that I am able to make a change—I can react differently right now in this moment."
>
> "Coach Your Self Up was a catalyst that has helped me become much more conscious of what I am doing with my life. This program has helped me become a better person."

In 2019, I partnered with an eLearning company (Interplicity) to create an online version of the Coach Your Self Up program. You can check that out at: coachyourselfup.com/course/paperback

Ever forward.

Introduction

Working with a coach can be powerful. "Coachees" experience professional and personal growth and transformation across multiple dimensions. However, not everyone has access to working with a skilled coach.

The idea of self-coaching came to me when I was describing my training program to others. I would summarize by saying, "Essentially I am teaching people how to coach themselves." My curiosity piqued, I did some research on the Internet and found several references to the self-coaching topic.

Most notably, I found another Bay Area resident, Ed Batista, an executive coach and an instructor at the Stanford Graduate School of Business (GSB). He has been blogging about self-coaching since 2009 and in the spring of 2015 offered a class called "The Art of Self-Coaching" as part of the Stanford GSB curriculum.

The inaugural class was a success and is now offered on an ongoing basis. Ed is publishing a book through Harvard Business Review (HBR) Press in 2018 entitled, *The Art of Self-Coaching*.

As you might imagine, I was thrilled to find there were others out there with this idea, and super-thrilled to hear that Ed Batista was going to have a book published on the subject with HBR Press.

Self-coaching is the next frontier of coaching.

It will never replace the importance or value of working with a skilled coach. However, for all the people who may never have that luxury, learning self-coaching skills can be a giant leap forward. The gift of self-coaching is invaluable.

There is no single "right" approach to self-coaching. As the field grows, numerous variations will make their way into the mix.

I get fired up when I think about the potential self-coaching holds for creating an exponential jump in self-awareness and the ability for large numbers of people to change behaviors and thought patterns that are limiting their potential at work and in their lives.

Given how much time the average person spends at work, it made sense to me to apply self-coaching in the career development arena, to use these powerful techniques to help individuals improve their effectiveness and overall success.

As an individual becomes more self-aware, she is positively impacted and starts making inroads to achieving more of her potential. This in turn has a positive effect on the individuals, groups and organizations with whom she interacts.

As individuals become more self-aware, their empathy for others generally increases. And as individuals practice more self-compassion, their compassion for others also rises.

I see a straight-line connection from rising levels of self-awareness and individuals continually aspiring to become better selves to creating more peaceful, loving, compassionate societies.

Narrowly, this work is about helping individuals be more successful in their careers and their lives. More broadly, it's about making a better world, one self-aware individual at a time.

Self-coaching is the **next frontier of coaching.**

About the Journey You are Embarking Upon

This book has been written in a way that roughly simulates the experience you would have if you were participating in the classroom version of the Coach Your Self Up® training program.

You will learn how to "coach yourself "to make sustainable behavioral changes that will have a positive impact on how you are "showing up" in your life.

Learn – Apply - Repeat
You will learn self-coaching concepts and techniques. Along the way I will encourage you to take a few breaks from the book and engage in Learning Practices to apply what you are learning. This significantly increases the odds that you will retain what you learn.

Keeping a Journal
I strongly recommend you keep a dedicated notepad or journal for this self-discovery journey. At various points throughout the book, mostly within the Learning Practices, there will be opportunities for you to capture your thoughts and reflections in writing.

Working with Others
This book will support you in working on your own or with others. When I teach this to groups inside organizations, I assign individuals to an "accountability team" with other participants. If you have one or more colleagues or friends who are interested in working through this process with you, you could work through the material together as accountability partners.

Book Structure

The content is laid out such that it builds on itself in a logical and easy-to-follow manner. I suggest that you work through the book from front to back.

Chapter 1 lays the foundation with supporting ideas, theories and philosophies from numerous fields of study.

Chapter 2 focuses on the topic of Managing Attention. I consider this a superpower for life. Many of you will never experience your attention the same way again after reading this chapter.

Chapter 3 contains the first set of Learning Practices where you will experiment with various aspects of managing your attention.

Chapter 4 is where you will learn about self-limiting behaviors (SLBs) and choose one of your own SLBs to work on.

Chapter 5 introduces the idea of "stories." You will learn about the Ladder of Inference and how we are wired to generate stories.

Chapter 6 contains the second set of Learning Practices where you will continue to practice managing your attention. You will also begin self-observing your selected SLB and noticing stories.

Chapter 7 provides insightful activities to help you more fully appreciate the idea of stories.

Chapter 8 lays out an approach on how to challenge your stories.

Chapter 9 introduces the idea of "deep" stories and encourages you to consider what some of your own deep stories might be.

Chapter 10 contains the third set of Learning Practices. You will continue to self-observe your SLB. You will also continue to look out for stories, including those that are associated with your SLB.

Chapter 11 introduces a Self-Observation Worksheet and provides multiple examples of how individuals have used self-coaching techniques to drive behavior change.

Chapter 12 shows how to use the self-coaching tools to work through situations where you feel "stuck."

Chapter 13 is where you will identify how you will maintain momentum and commit to a personal action plan to do so.

Chapter 1

Laying the Foundation

Let's start your self-coaching journey by introducing some important concepts that underlie this work.

Personal Development *is* Career Development

While this idea (that personal development is career development) is not yet mainstream, I believe it is simply a matter of time.

I think that a robust approach to career development has three main pillars. They are (1) identifying career goals and/or a vision, (2) developing technical/functional skills, and (3) working on behaviors and thought patterns.

1 - Identifying Career Goals and/or a Vision
In order to engage in meaningful career development efforts, it is helpful to set goals and honestly assess where you want to go. Many organizations have this pillar reasonably well covered and provide career development plans where employees can document their goals and discuss them with their managers.

2 - Developing Technical/Functional Skills
In some organizations, developing technical/functional skills is referred to as working on "the what" of your career development (i.e., "what" you do). This may start with a gap analysis to determine where you are today vs. where you aspire to be—your stated career goals or vision. This may also include identification of your strengths that you can leverage.

Gaps and strengths become the fodder for identifying appropriate development actions. For instance, you may need to deepen your skill set with certain platforms or tools. Or you may need to broaden your understanding of other parts of your department to become more holistic in your thinking and planning. Regardless of the particulars, the main point is for you to create a plan—and execute on it—to close those skill-based gaps and leverage your skill-based strengths.

3 - Working on Behaviors and Thought Patterns

Some organizations refer to working on behaviors and thought patterns as working on "the how" of your career development (i.e., "how" you do what you do). Tying back to the premise of this section, I see this pillar as personal development, or development of the self.

Of the three pillars, this one often gets the least amount of attention and support within organizations.

I believe this is tied to the still somewhat prevalent idea that personal development is only applicable outside the realm of the workplace. It's "personal," hence not "business." This is an outdated philosophy that needs to be further challenged. The world continues to change rapidly and it's time for this facet of career development to have its day in the sun.

Other than identifying your career goals and/or a career vision, the one thing you can control is how you "show up" at work. This includes how you behave, how you interact with others, how you manage yourself, and so on.

Personal development—learning more about and working with/on yourself—is intensely important to taking ownership of your professional path, regardless of your specific career goals. That could make self-coaching a potent cornerstone of the next generation of career development. I dare say that you are ahead of the curve on this one.

Your Most Important Coach—You

Odds are, you have at least one person in your life that you would consider some form of coach. This might be a friend, a colleague, a family member, a boss, etc. And maybe you have been fortunate enough to work with a professional coach in some capacity.

Coaches are helpful in many ways. When I ask people what they see as attributes of a good coach, common responses include:

- "He encourages me to pursue my goals."
- "She helps me to look at different perspectives."
- "He cares about me and my well-being."
- "She challenges my thinking."
- "He helps me find the answers that are already within me."
- "She supports me in becoming a better me."

Of course, there are many other attributes of good coaches, but this is a solid list. And as a professional coach, I believe it is of great value for you to have one or more coaches in your life.

That said, who do you talk to more than anybody else? This is not a trick question, and to the best of my knowledge, the answer is the same for all or almost all of us. We talk to *ourselves* more than anybody else. (And for those of you hearing that voice inside your head that's saying, "I don't know what he's talking about." That's the self-talk I am referring to.)

You are your most important coach. This is often an overlooked and hence under-utilized internal resource or capability.

YOUR MOST
IMPORTANT COACH

NOT **YOUR ONLY COACH**

How cool would it be to cultivate an inner coaching voice to bring to some of those conversations you already have with yourself?

To encourage you.

To challenge you.

To help you see different perspectives.

To help you become a better you.

That, in a nutshell, is what Coach Your Self Up is all about.

This is not about replacing the other coaches in your life. The ability to coach one's self is simply additive to this mix. In fact, while a bit oxymoronic, the most effective self-coaching will involve the support of others.

Self-Awareness—Turning on the Light

As we've noted, I believe the best thing you can do to drive your career success is to commit to your ongoing personal development—to deepen your self-awareness in pursuit of becoming a version of yourself that you aspire to be.

You can't stumble your way in the dark to your best self. You need to turn on the light. (I heard this phrase from a fellow Coach Your Self Up facilitator Pete Small—and I instantly took to it.)

We have known for a long time that self-awareness is important. The phrase "know thyself" dates back to one of the Seven Sages of Ancient Greece, Thales of Miletus[1]—around 2,500 years ago!

Businesses recognize the value of self-awareness as evidenced by their investment in leadership development programs and executive coaching engagements—both of which typically emphasize increasing self-awareness.

Coach Your Self Up makes this key aspect of leadership development available more broadly, well beyond the leadership suite. If we know that self-awareness plays such a pivotal part in being a successful leader in the workplace, why not start helping all employees in this arena much earlier in their careers?

There are additional more recent workplace trends that are shining a spotlight on the value of self-awareness. Here are just a few:

- Emotional Intelligence (EQ) includes self-awareness as a core pillar.
- Mindfulness places an emphasis on being self-aware in the present moment. (While the concept of mindfulness is thousands of years old, it has only recently begun to become more mainstream.)
- Conscious Capitalism and other flavors of Conscious Business pay homage to the importance and value of having "conscious" leaders and employees.

---

[1] Richard E. Boyatzis (2007), Interpersonal Aesthetics: Emotional and Social Intelligence Competencies are Wisdom. In Eric H. Kessler (ed.) and James R. Bailey (ed.) *Handbook of Organizational and Managerial Wisdom* (pp 223-242). Thousand Oaks, CA: Sage.

You can't stumble your way in the dark to your **best self.** You need to turn on the light.

The realm of self-awareness is enormous. For our work, we will emphasize three primary areas.

The first area is your **attention**—what you focus on and how well you maintain that focus. You are no doubt aware that your attention is constantly under attack by myriad information streams in our digital era, not to mention the many and various items on your internal "to do" list screaming to be heard. Learning to "take back" your attention—first by "paying attention to your attention," and then by learning to better harness and direct it—is instrumental to this work.

The second area is your **self-limiting behaviors**—things that you do (or don't do) that limit your success. You may be aware of one or more of your self-limiting behaviors ("Omg, I can't believe I just interrupted again, why can't I just stop doing that?"), or maybe they live in your blind spot. You will learn how to make sustainable shifts to these behaviors, even those that have been with you for years or even decades.

The third area is your **self-limiting stories**—thoughts that you have that limit your success. Stories (e.g., assumptions, opinions, conclusions, beliefs) are everywhere and many of us don't see them. An important part of Coach Your Self Up is helping you to see the sea of stories that you are swimming in and giving you simple ways to bust through stories that are getting in your way.

Target Outcomes—Tools for Creating Positive Shifts

Creating positive shifts is the primary overarching outcome that Coach Your Self Up delivers. You will learn a set of techniques and skills that allow you to make sustainable behavioral changes that will have a positive impact on your success.

> While the emphasis of Coach Your Self Up is to apply self-coaching skills to improve your success at work, the approach you will learn here is applicable in all facets of your life.

You will learn a set of techniques and skills that allow you to make sustainable behavioral changes that will have a positive impact on **your success**.

There are several other outcomes you are likely to experience that support this overarching outcome. These are highlighted below.

Shifts in one of your own Self-Limiting Behaviors (SLBs): This is a "work" book. To be most effective, you will begin to apply self-coaching techniques to one of your own selected self-limiting behaviors. This brings the concepts and techniques to life via practical hands-on application.

Improved Attention Management: Utilizing increased control over your attention, you will cultivate the ability to focus it when needed and, maybe more importantly, to notice when it has "wandered off" and needs to be "brought back."

Increased Emotional Intelligence (Self-Awareness and Empathy): By paying more focused attention to yourself, your self-awareness will expand. As you become more *self-aware* of your behaviors, stories, and feelings, your *empathy* for the perspectives and feelings of others is also likely to increase. As you practice self-compassion, it is probable that you will become more compassionate with others as well.

Enhanced Interpersonal Relationships: Seeing how your stories can negatively impact relationships, you will be able to develop and manage relationships more objectively.

Better Decisions: Learning to make conscious/aware decisions in the moment and not succumb to habitual/reflexive responses. Note the old adage that, "You cannot control what happens to you, but you can control how you respond."

Improved ability to coach others: Applying some of the self-coaching skills and techniques to coaching others around you.

Improved ability to be coached: When others are coaching you in the future, you are likely to be more open and receptive to the process, enabling you to make progress more quickly.

I have found that each individual that goes through this process experiences a unique set of benefits. While I believe that each person experiences some shift in each of the listed Target Outcomes, different outcomes tend to be more pronounced for different people.

I cannot tell you which one or two of these outcomes will be most prominent for you. Be open to see what unfolds as you do the work.

The Underlying Science

Some people see self-awareness work as soft or fluffy. It is anything but. Coach Your Self Up is specifically based on the latest research from the fields of cognitive psychology, neuroscience, and behavioral science.

Let's imagine that inside each of our heads there is a computer running that has a huge influence on how we experience the world and how we show up in the world. Of course, each of these computers is totally unique.

So here we are, each of us with this computer running in the background, often without being aware of it and with zero documentation. There is no user manual to help us look at and understand this computer. When is it serving us? When is it causing us to get in our own way?

The only way to figure this out is to start trying to observe how it operates, to catch it while it is running and see what it is doing. This can be challenging, because parts of this computer are operating subconsciously. One goal in Coach Your Self Up is to begin to bring this computer further into the light of our awareness, so that we can observe what it is up to.

This is where science has much to offer. Here is a brief overview.

The software component of this computer is our *mind*. Psychology is the study of our minds, and there is significant research that highlights how we can modify our thinking patterns to help us change our behaviors.

The hardware component of this computer is our *brain*. Neuroscience is the study of our brains. Recent findings in the realm of neuroplasticity show that the brain is in fact malleable, that we are not "hard-wired" as we had believed for such a long time. The human ability to create new neural pathways is an important part of Coach Your Self Up.

And finally, from a Behavioral Science perspective, we utilize something called the *Intentional Change Theory.*[2] Research shows we are more likely to make and sustain a behavioral shift if it is in the service of becoming a more ideal version of our self—as opposed to trying to fix something about our current self.

We are not broken people. We are all humans, experiencing our human lives, with our human shortcomings, aspiring to be better versions of ourselves.

Rest assured, the concepts you will discover through Coach Your Self Up have been substantiated through multiple fields in the domain of human performance and effectiveness.

Response-ability

Response-ability is being able to choose an appropriate response in-the-moment—not succumbing to your reflexive/habitual patterns.

The intent is to try new responses in those situations where you believe your current responses (patterns, habits) are not serving you and/or are getting in your way. You are not trying to determine the perfect response, nor are you trying to determine an average (what would everyone else do?) or compromise type of response. You are simply seeking a response that is better for you than your more typical response.

By experimenting with new responses, you will become more adept, over time, at being response-able.

---

[2] Richard E. Boyatzis and Kleio Akrivou, *The ideal self as the driver of intentional change* (Journal of Management Development, Vol. 25 No. 7, 2006. pp 624-642)

Coach Your Self Up helps you cultivate a set of practices that will make you more **response-able.**

Working Through the Book

This book is structured into bite-sized learning chunks which makes the content easier to absorb.

Your success in learning and applying these new skills will increase as you engage in Learning Practices at key junctures along the way. These practices, through direct experience and reflection, allow you to reinforce some of the key ideas and techniques that you are learning about.

Since our focus is on developing your awareness, this format is essential. There MUST be time for you to pay attention to and learn about yourself in order to move to a new place of readiness for the next set of ideas and techniques.

In an ideal world, you would spend about 30 minutes per week on the Learning Practices if you are doing this on your own, or an hour per week if you are working with others. The extra time when working with others is for weekly check-in discussions.

If you are interested in a more detailed overview of the content that will be covered in each chapter, refer to the section entitled "Book Structure" in the Introduction (page ix).

Small Shifts Lead to Big Changes

Another foundational concept that is important to understand is that "small shifts lead to big changes." It is quite common for us to shy away from making changes to our behaviors, especially behaviors that we have been exhibiting for a long time. It can feel like it will require a huge shift that will demand a huge amount of effort on our part. This often leads us to quit before we start.

Yes, creating change takes effort, but it does not need to be as hard as we think it will be. This is a classic story (that it will be too hard) we tell ourselves.

Think about a meteor that is on a collision course with Earth. Scientists believe (and I hope they are right!) that if we detect such a meteor, we can send a spacecraft to intercept the meteor and with a well-placed large explosion, knock it ever-so-slightly off its current path. This slight change in its trajectory will ultimately result in the meteor not just missing the Earth but missing the Earth by miles.

Likewise, you can think about your career and your life as being on some trajectory. Imagine time as the horizontal axis and your "potential realized" on the vertical.

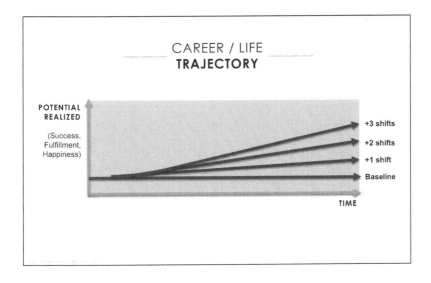

Going back to the meteor metaphor, with relatively small shifts in your awareness and behavior, that trajectory could shift in a positive way, leading to opportunities for you to continue to realize more of your potential.

For example, think of a person who has a self-limiting behavior of frequently interrupting others. It is pretty easy to imagine what that person's "trajectory" will look like if he doesn't work on that self-limiting behavior. It is also pretty easy to imagine a positive (upward) shift in that trajectory if he starts to make small shifts toward becoming a better listener. How much more of his potential will that person have realized in six months? A year? Five years?

Do you believe that more interesting career opportunities are likely to present themselves to "the better listener" version of the person vs. "the frequent interrupter" version?

I ask managers to think about two different employees, each of them having tendencies to interrupt others. I have them imagine one employee making small shifts toward being a better listener while the other employee does not. Responses are unanimous that the person who is working to become a better listener will be the beneficiary of more desirable development opportunities.

This is an important point of emphasis. If you believe, as I do and as a lot of research supports, that how you show up and how you behave and interact with others has a big impact on your career and life opportunities, then Coach Your Self Up gives you more control of your trajectory!

You are bending your future towards realizing more of your potential with each of these small shifts in your behavior.

(I *love* the phrase "bending your future" and the imagery it conjures up. I want to acknowledge that I first heard this from Jeremy Hunter, Ph.D., Founding Director of the Executive Mind Leadership Institute and Associate Professor of Practice at the Peter F. Drucker Graduate School of Management, Claremont Graduate University.)

You are **bending your future** towards realizing more of your potential with each of these small shifts in your behavior.

Using Our Minds to Change Our Brains

You are likely familiar with an old adage that, "You can't teach an old dog new tricks." In a related vein, you will hear people say things like, "Well, that's just the way I am" or, "I'm just wired that way and there's nothing I can do about it." And that feels true to us.

However, there is significant scientific evidence that our brain patterns are anything but hard-wired. The term that describes this phenomenon is neuroplasticity, or brain plasticity. (The Neuroplasticity entry on Wikipedia is a great jumping-off point if you want to know more - en.wikipedia.org/wiki/neuroplasticity)

Neuroplasticity shows that our brains can create new neural pathways that support the development of new patterns and associated habits.

Although psychologists have long believed that individuals could make significant changes to their thinking and behavioral patterns (behavior therapy has its roots in the 1920s), the neuroscience community continued to believe that the brain stopped developing after a certain point in late childhood. Sure, the neuroscientist community said, a person could modify their behavior. But they didn't believe that later-in-life behavioral change correlated to any physical changes in the brain.

It wasn't until the 1970s that the growing body of evidence led the neuroscience community to shift their position and embrace the idea of neuroplasticity. Study after study was showing that adult brains were *physically* changing...all the time!

Dr. Norman Doidge is a psychiatrist who has authored multiple books on the latest developments of neuroscience. In September of 2008, he was one of the speakers at an event sponsored by The Melbourne Conversations Program entitled "Your Brain: How it can change, develop and improve." Here is his opening statement:

"The idea that the brain is plastic in the sense of changeable, adaptable, malleable...is, I have come to believe, the single most important change in our understanding of the human brain in 400 years. It's revolutionary."

That is a heady (no pun intended) statement.

Rick Hanson is a psychologist who writes and teaches about the essential inner skills of personal well-being and personal growth. He has done a lot of work on the integration of topics from the fields of neuroscience and psychology.

In a talk that Rick gave at The Hudson Institute of Coaching's annual conference in 2014, he said:

"With a bit of skillful knowledge, we can use our minds to change our brains to change our minds for the better. This is called self-directed neuroplasticity."

You may need to read that one slowly a few times to let it sink in. His point is that just being aware of neuroplasticity causes some shifts in our minds. We become more open to the possibility that we actually can make changes in areas where we used to think it was not possible. (Along these lines, there is a fun statement I've heard a few times: "Neuroplasticity is a six-syllable word for hope.")

What becomes possible for you knowing that you can create new neural pathways, that your brain can be "reprogrammed?"

Prior to 2005, you would have been hard-pressed to learn about this concept unless your profession required you to do so.

The fact that we are not *hard-wired*, but in fact are *soft-wired*, has huge implications for all of us as a species. This is not lost on many in the field (including Doidge and Hanson) and since 2005 there have been several books published on this topic targeted at a mainstream audience. (See the Resources section at the back of this book for a list of some of those books.)

Just being aware that neuroplasticity exists (and believing it), is sufficient understanding for Coach Your Self Up.

Cultivating a Growth Mindset

I mentioned earlier that we have the equivalent of a computer running in our heads 24/7. The hardware of that computer is the brain and the software is the mind.

Neuroplasticity is a helpful concept pertaining to the *brain* that supports our approach to self-coaching. Let's now look at a helpful concept pertaining to the *mind* that is also supportive of our approach. It is all about "mindset."

Carol Dweck, a well-known psychologist at Stanford University, has articulated the difference between what she calls a "fixed" mindset and a "growth" mindset[3]. Here is a brief summation of how she defines these two mindsets.

A person with a *fixed mindset* believes his intelligence, personality, and character are carved in stone; that his potential is fixed. This person rarely achieves anywhere close to his full potential.

Conversely, a person with a *growth mindset* believes that his intelligence, personality, and character can be developed; that his potential is unknown (and unknowable). This person continues to reach ever-higher levels of his potential.

There are a few areas where it is helpful to see how people with these differing mindsets behave. Please read through the table on the following page and think about where you typically fall on these different dimensions.

---

[3] Carol S. Dweck, *Mindset* (New York: Ballantine Books, 2006).

	FIXED MINDSET	**GROWTH MINDSET**
IT'S UP TO YOU!	Believe that my intelligence, personality and character are carved in stone; my potential is determined at birth.	Believe that my intelligence, personality and character can be developed! A person's true potential is unknown (and unknowable).
DESIRE	Look smart in every situation and prove myself over and over again. Never fail!	Stretch myself, take risks and learn. Bring on the challenges!
EVALUATION OF SITUATIONS	Will I succeed or fail? Will I look smart or dumb?	Will this allow me to grow? Will this help me overcome some of my learning edges?
DEALING WITH SETBACKS	I'm a failure (identity). I'm an idiot.	I failed (action). What did I learn that I can apply in the future?
CHALLENGES	Avoid challenges; get defensive or give up easily.	Embrace challenges; persist in the face of setbacks.
EFFORT	Why bother? It's not going to change anything.	Growth and learning require effort.
CRITICISM	Ignore constructive criticism.	Learn from criticism. How can I improve?
SUCCESS OF OTHERS	Feel threatened by the success of others. If you succeed, then I fail.	Finds lessons & inspiration in the success of others.
RESULT...	Plateau early; achieve less than my full potential.	Reach ever-higher levels of achievement.

As you look over these descriptors, what most resonates with you? Would you acknowledge that you have a fixed mindset? Or do you believe you have more of a growth mindset?

You likely see yourself as having some of both. This is not a binary thing where you are one or the other. Look at this as a continuum between the two poles of fixed mindset and growth mindset. There may be some dimensions where you tend to embrace more of a growth mindset than others. For example, maybe you are comfortable embracing setbacks, yet have a hard time with constructive criticism.

You tend to operate from a default location on each of the continuums shown in the table on the prior page. In certain situations, you may have a tendency to move further along the continuum(s) in one direction or the other.

For example, even individuals who typically embrace setbacks as learning opportunities (growth mindset) can periodically have setbacks that make them feel like a failure (fixed mindset).

For most of us, cultivating a growth mindset is not easy. It takes ongoing effort. The starting point, as with so many aspects of this work, is awareness.

Just being aware of the fixed/growth mindset concept helps you to get a stronger sense of where your current default mindset falls on the continuum. Being aware that a fixed mindset will limit you in achieving your potential will hopefully trigger you to take steps toward developing more growth mindset tendencies.

The goal is to become more aware of your mindset and, over time, work to move toward the growth mindset side of the continuum.

More organizations are espousing the benefits of a growth mindset as part of their desired culture. I imagine you can see how cultivating a growth mindset would serve you in your career.

The self-coaching approach you will learn in Coach Your Self Up requires that you generally embrace and embody a growth mindset. If you lean towards a fixed mindset, consider using Coach Your Self Up to help you start shifting towards a growth mindset.

Coach Your Self Up requires that you generally embrace and embody a **growth mindset**.

Moving through Levels of Learning Engagement[4]

In addition to being aware of the differences between a fixed mindset and a growth mindset, awareness of what I call "levels of learning engagement" can be helpful in getting the most out of Coach Your Self Up. (Note that this concept can be helpful to you in your work when learning *anything* new.)

In theory, individuals move in and through these levels during any learning experience. While movement can be linear, with some amount of time spent in each level, it is also common to bounce around from any level to any other level very quickly.

Levels of Learning Engagement

COMMITMENT	I'm *committed* to put in the necessary effort to achieve <this outcome> which will serve me.
BELIEF	I *believe* I can achieve <this outcome> which will serve me.
ASPIRATION	I would *like* to achieve <this outcome> which will serve me.
CURIOSITY	I wonder how this might serve me?

Level 1 – Curiosity
This level is characterized by an interest in learning more. You have not identified anything specific you want to get out of the learning experience, but you intentionally remain open-minded to seeing what might come up for you.

Level 2 – Aspiration
This level is characterized by having identified at least one specific outcome you hope to realize from the learning experience. You are

---

[4] Distilled from self-efficacy theories originating with: Bandura, Albert *Social Learning Theories*. City: Prentice-Hall, 1976. Print

not sure it is possible, but you hope it is. You keep this aspiration in mind as a way to stay engaged with the learning experience.

Level 3 – Belief

This stage is characterized by believing that the learning experience will help you achieve one or more of the specific outcomes you aspire to. You may feel excitement when you shift into this state, as this target outcome now feels realistic and attainable. You may move quickly from Belief to Commitment.

Level 4 – Commitment

This level is characterized by simply committing to "doing whatever it takes" to achieve your desired outcome. You are engaged with the learning experience.

It can be common for individuals at any level to "exit/give up" on the learning experience. For example, a person at Level 4 might say "I am no longer committed to this, so I am done." If you find yourself no longer resonating with the level at which you were operating, try to re-anchor yourself on a lower level. For example, if you are at Level 4 and no longer feel committed…

…Ask yourself: "Do I still believe this can help me achieve my desired outcome?" If yes, re-anchor at Level 3. If no…

…Ask yourself: "Do I still aspire to achieve at least one specific outcome from this work?" If yes, re-anchor at level 2. If no…

…Challenge yourself to remain curious and open-minded to continue on with the work.

Hopefully you will find yourself at Level 2 from the get-go and will be able to move to Level 3 or 4 fairly quickly.

On the Self-Coaching Path

My schooling as an engineer taught me that it is helpful to have a process to bring concepts to life, to make them actionable. To that end there is a simple three-step process called the self-coaching path. You will find a graphic depiction of the self-coaching path on the following page.

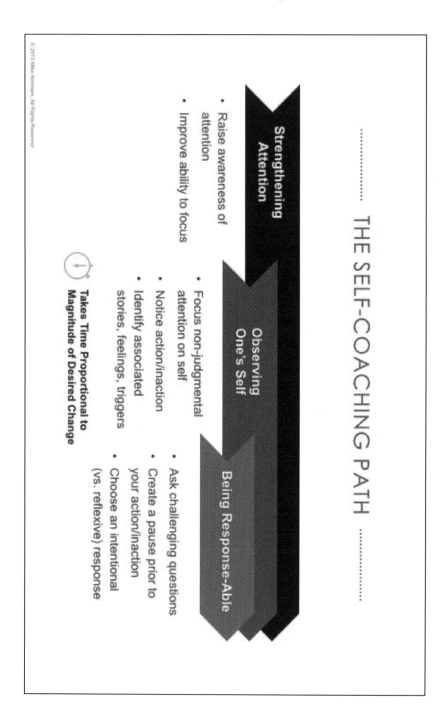

THE SELF-COACHING PATH

Strengthening Attention
- Raise awareness of attention
- Improve ability to focus

Observing One's Self
- Focus non-judgmental attention on self
- Notice action/inaction
- Identify associated stories, feelings, triggers

Being Response-Able
- Ask challenging questions
- Create a pause prior to your action/inaction
- Choose an intentional (vs. reflexive) response

Takes Time Proportional to Magnitude of Desired Change

Step 1 – Strengthening Attention

The first step involves becoming more skilled in the baseline ability to more effectively manage your attention. I have a talk that I give entitled "Managing Attention – A Superpower for Life." I really do see this as a superpower.

For many of us, our attention is typically something that just is. We follow our attention, but we don't often think about what it is doing.

You will start by becoming more aware of your attention. This is an important aspect of learning to control it more effectively.

Step 2 – Observing One's Self

Once you begin to improve your ability to manage your attention, you will be able to focus your attention on yourself more effectively. This feeds into the second step of the self-coaching path, which is to cultivate a self-observation practice.

Most of us are less skilled in self-observation than we tend to believe. Until you are able to cultivate a strong practice of self-observation, it will be difficult if not impossible to make sustainable changes in behavior.

Witnessing ourselves through a neutral, non-judgmental third-party lens is important. While difficult, we need to learn to be impartial with ourselves. Otherwise, the weight of our self-criticism can become an obstacle to our ability to make a desired change.

An important skill is being able to simply notice our action (or inaction)—helping us to be more aware of our behavior.

After you have developed heightened awareness around your (in)action, you can begin to:

- Identify any of your *stories* that are associated with your (in)action. Look for themes if you see multiple stories.
- Identify any *feelings* that are associated with your (in)action.
- Identify if there are any *triggers* that precede your (in)action.

It is important to note this process takes time. The more ingrained the behavior is that we are trying to change, the more time we need to spend really noticing and understanding what's going on.

Step 3 – Being Response-Able

Earlier in this chapter we discussed the concept of response-ability. The third step of the self-coaching path is bringing that to life. You will become more and more response-able; able to more consistently choose responses in-the-moment as opposed to succumbing to your more habitual ways of responding or reacting.

Professional coaches ask their clients challenging questions. With Coach Your Self Up, you will learn to ask yourself challenging questions. You will ultimately be able to create a pause prior to engaging in your reflexive response, and proactively choose your response—to act in a non-habitual, more "present" way.

We will revisit the self-coaching path numerous times.

Accepting that Change Takes Time

Most of us want to fix things quickly. "If I have a particular behavior that is getting in my way, let me fix it ASAP and just move on."

The challenge with the quick-fix approach is that it often yields a surface level fix and does not get at the underlying issues going on inside of us. Hence the behavior or habitual pattern often returns.

A simple example to illustrate this pertains to New Year's resolutions. In the last few years I have made a practice of getting into the gym for a brief workout, four days per week. I brace myself in early January for the influx of individuals that have made a New Year's resolution to work out more regularly. By mid-January or early February, most of those new faces have disappeared. It is difficult to proclaim you are making an "outer" change and make it stick without doing the needed "inner" work.

The challenge with the quick-fix approach is that it often yields a surface level fix and **does not get at the underlying issues going on inside of us**. Hence the behavior or habitual pattern often returns.

If a person were using the self-coaching path to create a new habit of going to the gym, she would spend ample time self-observing, just noticing what was going on when she decided to *not go* to the gym. Gaining a deep understanding of that inner context would lay the foundation for making an internal shift that would support the "outer" shift of getting into the gym more regularly.

Our behavioral patterns are patterns for a reason. They are often years, if not decades, in the making.

It is important to do the "inner" work (i.e., work on our mindset and our stories) to make and sustain "outer" behavioral changes. The self-coaching path was designed to ensure you have the tools to do the important inner work that awaits you.

CHAPTER 1 SUMMARY

Laying the Foundation

- Personal development *is* career development.

- You are your most important coach. You will cultivate an inner coaching voice to bring to some of your ongoing conversations with yourself.

- We have known for thousands of years that self-awareness is important.

- We are focused on increasing self-awareness in three areas—attention, self-limiting behaviors, and stories.

- The primary target outcome of this book is giving you a blueprint and tools for creating positive shifts in your life.

- Response-ability is being able to choose an appropriate response in-the-moment.

- Small shifts lead to big changes. With each small shift, you are "bending your future" toward achieving more of your potential.

- Neuroplasticity shows that we are not hard-wired. We can create new neural pathways to support new ways of being.

- Self-coaching requires that you embrace a growth mindset—believing that your potential is not fixed.

- There are four levels of learning engagement, from "curiosity" to "commitment." If you disengage, try to stay curious.

- The self-coaching path is the model that brings self-coaching to life. The three steps include: (1) strengthening attention, (2) observing one's self, and (3) being response-able.

- Sustainable behavior change takes time. You need to do the "inner" work to support the "outer" change.

Chapter 2

Managing Attention - A Superpower for Life

Coach Your Self Up is built upon raising self-awareness. In this chapter I introduce a cool and powerful aspect of self-awareness which has to do with *managing attention*. I see this as a superpower for life. (Lest the double entendre not jump out at you, this is a superpower for living, and a superpower you can use for the rest of your life.)

It should be noted that managing attention is an important component of mindfulness practices that are rooted in Buddhist teachings that are thousands of years old.

Benefits

While this started with an intention to help people improve their self-observation skills, it quickly became apparent that there were many other benefits associated with managing one's attention.

First, it helps you to be more present, i.e., in the current moment. Pam McLean, the leader of the Hudson Institute of Coaching, refers to presence as a superpower. The path to presence and the power it brings is through managing attention.

Beyond that, managing attention can help us improve our ability to focus. It can help improve our productivity.

It can also help us improve relationships as we become more present with and attentive to others. And it helps with improving key facets of our Emotional Intelligence—awareness of both self and others.

As I stepped back and looked at this potent list of benefits, I thought, "There really is a superpower here."

If you are able to start making small shifts in managing your attention, that alone could help you tremendously in your career.

Superpower Defined

Here is how I define the superpower of Managing Attention: the ability to direct or control your attention on demand.

The superpower of Managing Attention is the ability to direct or control your attention **on demand.**

Here are a few skills that will help you develop the superpower:

- Being able to notice when your attention has drifted and gently bringing it back to where you want it to be.
- Having the ability to transport yourself to the present moment on demand.

Challenges to Paying Attention

What are some key challenges that make it hard for you to focus your attention?

Common responses to this question include "email," "text messages," "chat messages," "having so much to do," "thinking about <stuff>," and so forth. I imagine that some of those responses may have come up as you thought about the question.

It is hard to focus our attention as we live in a fast-moving world where there are often multiple items vying for it.

In their 2016 book *The Distracted Mind: Ancient Brains in a High-Tech World* [5] , Adam Gazzaley and Larry D. Rosen describe these phenomena as "goal interference." This phrase is based on the premise that we have a "goal" for where we would like to focus our attention. "Goal interference" is anything that vies for our attention and impacts our ability to remain focused on the object which is the desired "goal."

My comments below are based heavily on this work of Gazzaley and Rosen. And for simplicity I will use the word "interference" as a synonym for "goal interference."

Interference comes at us both externally and internally. And there is a distinction between a distraction and an interruption. In both cases, a *distraction* is something that you ignore (or attempt to ignore) while you carry on with your original goal. An *interruption* is when you decide to engage in the interference and multitask.

---

[5] Adam Gazzaley and Larry D. Rosen, *The Distracted Mind – Ancient Brains in a High-Tech World* (Cambridge, MA: The MIT Press, 2017).

Here are some examples:

You are having a one-on-one conversation with a colleague at lunch and giving her your focused attention. Your phone buzzes in your pocket (*external distraction*). You choose to ignore it. You have a thought: "Oh that reminds me, I need to follow up with my partner on our dinner plans" (*internal distraction*) and you decide to let that thought go and stay focused on your colleague.

Your phone buzzes again. This time you look at it and tell your friend, "Let me check this…. keep talking, I'm listening" (*external interruption*). A bit later you again start thinking about what your dinner plans will be with your partner and start to work on that mentally while still listening to your friend (*internal interruption*).

Do *not* underestimate the power of gaining more control over your attention, especially in this ADD culture we live in where we are constantly bombarded with stimuli, with our brains "learning" to skitter our attention all over the place all day long.

Let's Play with Our Attention

Given the importance of attention, many of us spend way too little time learning about it. Most of us operate on the surface of attention. Let's get underneath the surface and learn a bit more about it.

The concepts below are based on the work of Gary Sherman, author of *Perceptual Integration – The Mechanics of Awakening*[6]. Gary has been teaching self-awareness and meditation for over 35 years. I am grateful to Gary for allowing me to use his material.

Please play along here as I offer you a chance to experience your attention in a new way. This will be *much* more powerful and insightful for you if you do these activities.

---

[6] Gary Sherman, *Perceptual Integration – The Mechanics of Awakening* (Cotati, CA: Inner Harmonics Press, 2013).

Activity 1 – Following Your Attention

I invite you to get comfortable wherever you are. This can be done sitting at your desk, sitting/standing on the bus/train, lying in your bed or on the ground, wherever you are.

For 30 seconds, with your eyes open, simply "follow" your attention. Don't try to control it—just let it go and follow it. You might want to set a timer, so you know when you have reached 30 seconds. Or you may be comfortable just "winging it" until you feel like you have put in enough time.

> Go ahead...30 seconds...follow your attention.

*****

Welcome back.

What did you experience?

How did that feel?

For some of you, it may be the first time you have ever forcibly paid attention to your attention, which can be a bit weird.

(And if you did not do the activity, stop reading and do it! It literally takes just 30 seconds.)

I assume you noticed that your attention was *moving*. It is constantly on the move, bouncing from one thing to another. If you followed the instructions and did not try to control it, you noticed that your attention moves without you.

Your attention is always moving, with or without your conscious involvement. We spend a significant amount of our waking hours on autopilot, not in control of our attention.

Slow down for a moment and let this sink in. *Your attention moves with or without you.* On the one hand, you knew this already. On the other hand, this is heady, profound stuff. This idea fascinated me when I first let it soak in.

Your attention moves *with* or *without* you.

Here is another question. Where did your attention land during that 30 seconds? While it is always moving, it tends to pause periodically on something before moving along.

Your attention is unique. When I lead this activity in a group setting, each individual's experience of their attention is unlike any other individual's. Since I do not know where you are doing this, I cannot even begin to speculate where your attention went.

However, I can tell you conceptually where it went. It moved to and through three different "locations."

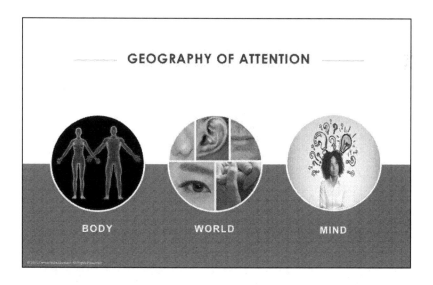

Location 1 – *Your Body*: Attention can focus on bodily sensations. Feeling warm or cold, feeling pain or an itch, feeling your breath in your abdomen or nostrils, feeling your feet on the floor.

Location 2 – *Your World*: Your attention can be in the world as experienced by you directly through your five senses. You can be focused on something you see, hear, smell, touch, or taste. (I refer to this as *your world* as it is based on your direct experience.)

Location 3 – *Your Mind*: Your attention can focus on your thoughts. "What am I having for dinner tonight?" "I can't believe I said that thing I said at the team meeting yesterday."

Think of these three locations as the "geography" or the "landscape" of attention. Awareness of this geography lays the foundation for more effectively managing your attention.

Let us consider how this new landscape correlates to the idea of being present. Consider the three locations (Body, World, Mind). Two of these locations can only be experienced in the present moment by your attention: *Body* and *World*. Think about it. It is impossible for you to experience your bodily sensations at any other time than the present moment. The same holds true for experiencing the world through your five senses.

While it is possible for you to have your attention in your *Mind* in the present moment, most of the time that we are in our minds we are thinking about the past or the future.

Bring your attention to your *body* or your *world* and you are **in the present moment**.

As noted earlier, the ability to bring yourself to the present moment "on demand" is a component of the Managing Attention superpower. You have just learned a way to do this! Bring your attention to your body or your world and you have brought yourself to the present moment.

Gary Sherman recommends always coming to the present moment through your body. This helps you to be more fully aware of your own presence.

For example, let's say you are sitting in a meeting and notice your mind has drifted off and you are thinking about your to-do list. Your intention is to bring your attention back to the meeting. Instead of immediately shifting your attention to the meeting, take just a few seconds to bring your attention to your body (e.g., feel your back against the chair, or your feet on the ground, or your breath), then quickly shift your attention to the person speaking.

Activity 2 – Labeling Where Your Attention Lands
I invite you to again get comfortable wherever you are. As with the first activity, I want you to follow your attention for another 30 seconds with your eyes open.

This time when it "lands" someplace, quickly mentally label the location (Body, World, Mind) where it has landed.

For example, you might hear a siren going by, and in that moment, you would mentally label your attention as being in the World.

You may notice yourself thinking "That sounds like an ambulance," which you label as Mind. You notice that your heart begins to beat faster (Body) which you attribute to a recent experience where a friend was in an accident (Mind). And so on…

> Go ahead…30 seconds…follow your attention and mentally label where it lands.

*****

39

Welcome back.

What did you experience?

How did that feel?

By starting to label where your attention lands, you are inserting conscious action into the process. Using the three locations within the geography of attention allows us to locate ourselves mentally.

We all know how to answer the question "Where are you?" based on our physical location. The geography of attention gives us an ability to answer the question "Where are you?" based on our mental "location." We have all been in meetings with people who were physically present, but were totally somewhere else mentally—in fact, this is common.

The key learning point from this activity is that by focusing your awareness on your attention, you are able to see which of these three mental locations you are in at any given moment.

You can **locate** your attention at any given moment.

Activity 3 – Intentionally Moving Your Attention Around
You have experienced first-hand, or witnessed, or you can try to imagine, the joy of floating down a stream on an inner tube. After a certain distance, hopping out of the stream, running back to the starting point, and jumping in to do it all over again.

The attention activities we are doing are analogous to this inner-tubing experience.

In the first activity, you simply floated down the stream of your attention, casually noticing the landscape as it went by.

In the second activity, you started over at the top of the stream and inserted some conscious control into the mix. You paid attention to, and labeled, the landscape as it went by. If you couldn't control where the "river" was taking you, you could at least name the landscape that the river of attention flowed through.

In this third activity, let's step back into the stream with a rudder, so you can take more control of the direction your attention takes.

Now you are going to *direct your attention* as opposed to *following* it. 45 seconds is more effective than 30 seconds for this activity. You will want to pick one of the three locations (Body, World, or Mind) and focus your attention there. After seven or eight seconds, choose another of the three locations and shift your focus there. Shift your attention five or six times in total.

You might start, for example, by choosing "Body." After seven or eight seconds, you might shift to "World." After seven or eight more seconds, you might shift to "Mind." And so on.

When you focus on your Body, choose <u>one</u> *bodily sensation* to concentrate on (your breath, your butt on the seat, your feet on the floor) until you shift to the next location.

When you focus on your World, choose <u>one</u> of your *senses* to concentrate on—something you see or hear or feel, etc.—until you shift to the next location.

When you focus on your Mind, go up into your *thoughts* and let them run free.

> Give it a try and see how it goes. With your eyes open, focus
> your attention on one location (Body, World, Mind) and then
> move it to another location (Body, World, Mind) every seven
> or eight seconds, a total of five or six times.

*****

Welcome back again.

What did you experience?

How did that feel?

It is typical in my experience with a group that they find this hard
to do. Even for a short timeframe, it can be difficult to hold one's
attention on one thing.

Even though it is difficult, the key learning point from this activity
is that it can be done. *We are able to control our attention.*

It is not easy. Just as we go to the gym to build body muscle, we need
to exercise our attention to strengthen it. The more we practice
managing our attention, the stronger our brain "muscles" get at
doing so.

*If you are interested in having a guided audio experience of these and many
other attention activities, check out Gary Sherman's free audio library on
this topic which is referenced in the Resources section at the back of this
book. There are 15 different topics of roughly 10-minutes each.*

You can **control** your attention. It is not easy. It **takes practice**.

Activity 4 – Focusing Your Attention on Your Body
Let's do a brief closed-eye meditation to focus on your body.

If you have some experience with meditation or already have a meditation practice, you can skip this activity. Or if you would like to drop in to a brief body-scan meditation at this time, feel free to do so. If you do not have much experience with meditation, please continue on with this activity.

I like this activity as it provides an opportunity to note that a key aspect of meditation is managing attention.

If you have access to the Internet, you can search for "guided meditation audio." You will find numerous options presented to you by your search engine. It should be easy to find something that is relatively brief (three to five minutes). I suggest choosing something that refers to "breathing" or "body scan."

Alternatively, you could read the script below and then close your eyes and do your best to follow the instructions from memory.

Paying Attention to Your Body – Meditation Script

"Close your eyes. Start by becoming aware that you even have a body. This is something that many of us have "forgotten" to a certain degree.

For posture, have both of your feet on the ground and sit up straight. Squeeze your hands into fists, raise your shoulders, squeeze your eyes shut, and take a deep breath in, as deep as you can... And then release, let go of all your tension, your breath flows all the way out, and you can sink down into your chair. Feel the weight of your body in your chair. You should be comfortable but not slouched over.

Now focus on your breathing.

First, become aware that you are breathing, and then pay attention to the process of breathing. You might prefer to focus your attention on your abdomen or your chest or wherever you "feel" the breath most strongly in your body. Or you might prefer to focus your attention on the air moving in and out of your nostrils. Notice that each breath is different from every other breath.

Some of you may find it helpful to count your breaths to help stay focused. I recommend counting backwards from 10. 10 on the in-breath, 9 on the out-breath, and so on. When you get to 1, start over at 10.

Every time you notice that your attention has wandered away from your breath, gently bring it back.

(Allow 1 minute of silence.)

Take a final deep breath or two and when you are ready, open your eyes and come back into the room."

Activity 5 – Focusing Your Attention on the World (Listening)
You need a partner for this activity. If you do not have somebody you can do this with, read through it to get an understanding of the common learning points that come up.

One of you will speak for one-and-a-half minutes, a monologue. If you run out of things to say, that's fine, just sit there in silence and whenever you have something to say again, continue speaking. The listener should simply listen. The listener can use facial expressions, nodding, etc., to show interest, but should not engage in dialogue.

You and your partner will take turns being the speaker and the listener. After you have each had a chance to do this, talk to each other briefly about what the experience was like as the speaker and as the listener.

When we debrief this activity in a group setting, one key theme typically emerges—that we are not as good at listening as we might have thought we were.

There are many reasons for this. A few common ones are:
- "I'm thinking ahead to what I'm going to say next."
- "I'm connecting to certain things the other person is saying and want to ask questions to learn more about that. I'm worried if I don't ask the question immediately I may forget to do so later."
- "I'm being distracted by external and/or internal stimuli."

Some tips for you to consider for improving your listening skills:
- Be *intentional* about focusing your attention on the other person. Be present with them.
- Be *curious* about what they have to say. (I have a post-it note staring me in the face every time I open my laptop. It says, "Be Curious." I cannot overstate the importance of cultivating this aspect of your mindset in helping you become a better listener.)
- *Trust* that if you listen with curiosity, you will have something appropriate to say or ask when the person is finished.

There are many resources out there to help people develop active or empathic listening skills. That is not the emphasis of this book. However, I'd be remiss not to touch on this important aspect of paying attention (listening), as it is really important and something that you engage in numerous times each day. Being a good listener is a skill that will help you in any work environment; it has a huge impact on your effectiveness and interpersonal relationships.

*****

When I first learned these principles of attention, I had a somewhat split reaction. Some of the ideas felt quite obvious, "Duh, I knew that." On the other hand, some of the same ideas felt profound. Taken together, I never saw my attention in the same way again.

In closing this chapter, I will reiterate that it is not easy to manage our attention. The important thing is to practice. The more that we practice doing so, the stronger our brain muscles get at it.

We don't practice managing our attention so that we will be able to control it all the time. We practice managing our attention so that we will **continue to get better at doing so**.

While we are on the subject of practice, we are ready to jump into the next chapter, which includes the first set of Learning Practices.

As mentioned in the Introduction, you can work through this book with one or more others—an accountability partner or partners. If you are doing that, here is some additional helpful information.

Working with Your Accountability Partner(s) (if applicable):

When working with others, I encourage you to meet one time for 30-minutes during the Learning Practices time windows.

Please read the following guidelines:

- Working with others increases the odds that you will engage in the Learning Practices and gain maximum benefit from Coach Your Self Up.

- Try to meet for 30-minutes during each of the Learning Practices time windows. Suggested discussion topics are provided for each meeting. Additional interaction is encouraged at your discretion.

- As a member of this group, you are making a commitment to yourself and to your accountability partner(s) that you will make these meetings a priority *even if* you haven't done your own work. Of course, the meetings will be much more valuable for all participants if you have all done your work.

- If one or more of you stops participating, carry on with those of you who are still committed to the work; even if that is just you.

CHAPTER 2 SUMMARY

Managing Attention – A Superpower for Life

- The superpower of Managing Attention is the ability to direct or control your attention on demand.

- If you are able to start making small shifts in managing your attention, that alone will help you tremendously in your career.

- We live in a fast-paced world with lots of stimuli vying for our attention. These stimuli act as "interference" to our attention.

- Interference comes in two flavors—distractions (when we ignore) and interruptions (when we engage).

- Attention is always moving. It moves *with or without* our conscious involvement.

- There are three locations that attention moves in and through: Body, World (via the five senses), Mind (thoughts). Think of this as a geography or landscape of attention.

- We can "locate" our attention within this geography at any time.

- We are able to control and direct our attention.

- Controlling attention is hard. It takes practice.

- Listening to others is an important skill that is rooted in managing attention.

Chapter 3

Learning Practices (First Set)

Welcome to the first set of Learning Practices.

Please take some time to step away from this book and engage with these practices. When I work with groups we take two weeks. You may prefer a bit less or a bit more time.

Engaging in these practices helps to solidify key learning points and will provide you with new insights that will deliver additional benefits when you come back to continue on with Chapter 4.

As you may recall from the Introduction, I recommend you keep a journal of your experiences with this work. There is power in writing things down and all three sets of Learning Practices provide suggested journaling activities.

If you are doing this on your own, it will take strong discipline on your part. Decide what tactics you will employ to ensure you stick with it. I personally do well with recurring calendar reminders.

Part I - Strengthening Attention

The following practices will help you raise awareness of your attention and start to increase your ability to manage it. You are cultivating the superpower.

Part IA – Bringing Yourself to the Present Moment for Five Minutes per Day

- Focus your attention on your bodily sensations or sensory perceptions of the world around you for at least five minutes per day. You might attempt this in one sitting or in shorter bursts (e.g., 10-30 seconds at a time) that add up to five minutes over the course of your day.

- This practice builds muscles in the brain and creates new neural pathways that over time will strengthen your ability to focus your attention on command.

- Choose one or more common tasks/activities as opportunities to practice focusing your attention. Here are some ideas to consider:
  o Participating in a group meeting
  o Participating in a one-on-one conversation
  o Commuting to work
  o Eating a meal
  o Working out
  o Taking a walk
  o Performing a mundane task (work) or chore (household)
  o Walking down the hall at work
  o Waking up and/or going to bed
  o Using the bathroom sink (e.g., washing, brushing teeth, shaving)
  o Taking a shower
  o Listening to music
  o Playing sports

You will be significantly better prepared for the next steps of the process if you take time to **engage with these learning practices**.

Part IB – Attending to Three Specific Experiences

- Choose three specific experiences from the list below where you will work to remain present by maintaining the focus of your attention on either your body or your sensory perceptions of the world around you. When you notice that your attention has wandered off, gently bring it back to the object (e.g., body, world) of your intended focus. If possible, choose at least one work-related experience.
  - o Participating in a group meeting
  - o Participating in a one-on-one conversation
  - o Commuting to work
  - o Eating a meal
  - o Working out
  - o Taking a walk
  - o Performing a mundane task (work) or chore (household)
  - o Just being ("Don't just do something, sit there!")
- Note that your attention muscles may be weak and holding your attention for extended periods of time can be taxing. Do your best to hold your attention for as long as possible, but do not force it—let yourself "off-the-hook" if you decide to let go of your intended focus sooner than you had hoped.

Journaling

For each of the three selected experiences, write a few sentences that describe your feelings and thoughts about the experience. Try to do this as soon after the experience as possible.

Reflect on and write about the following:

- What was the activity?
- What was the intended object of my attention?
- What was my sense of how far/long my attention drifted away prior to my noticing it and bringing it back?
- Did this experience bring about any feelings (e.g., frustration, happiness, etc.)?
- What insights did I glean from this experience that apply to my effectiveness at work?

Working with your Accountability Partner(s) (if applicable):
- Schedule your first 30-minute group conversation to take place during this Learning Practices time window.
- Meet in-person if it's easy for you to do so.

Here is an optional recommended discussion outline for your group conversation:
- Talk a bit about what each of you is **aspiring to get out of Coach Your Self Up.**
- Talk about **what each of you wants from this group** to help stay committed to this work.
- Discuss your **experiences with the Learning Practices.**
  - How are you doing with the "five minutes per day" activity?
  - How about the "three specific experiences?"
- **Determine if you want to do anything differently at your next Learning Practices meeting.** Each person briefly answers the following two questions:
  - What went well today that we want to continue?
  - What might we do next time to improve?

Summary of Learning Practices (First Set)

Part I – Strengthening Attention

- Part IA – Using your attention to bring yourself to the present moment for a total of five cumulative minutes per day
- Part IB – Paying attention to and journaling about three selected experiences

---

Good luck with these Learning Practices. I hope you enjoy them. "See you" back here for Chapter 4 when you are ready.

"Being Here" Activity

Managing Attention – Focus on Your Body

Sit up in your chair with both feet on the ground. You should be comfortable, but not slouched over. Take a few deep breaths.

With your eyes closed, breathe naturally and take just 30 seconds to focus your attention on your breath. You can bring your attention to your nostrils, your abdomen, wherever you find your breath most physically noticeable in your body.

Become aware of in-breath, out-breath, and the space in between. When you become distracted by a thought, a sound, or another bodily sensation, just acknowledge it, and gently let it go. Bring your attention back to your breath.

Allow 30 seconds.

When you are ready, take one last deep breath and gently open your eyes and come back into your space.

Chapter 4

Self-Limiting Behaviors (SLBs)

Welcome back.

Ideally, you have been "away" for a while, engaging in the Learning Practices from Chapter 3.

Before you dive in to this chapter, I invite you to take a minute and get a bit more *present* by engaging in the "Being Here" activity on the prior page. You will practice using your superpower of managing attention to focus on your breath, a bodily sensation. This will help to get you "here" mentally.

Journaling - Learning Practices - Reflection

Let's take a few minutes to reflect on your recent experiences.

- Jot down a few sentences with your high-level thoughts and/or feelings about your experiences with the Learning Practices. Are you more aware of your attention? Are you more aware of when your attention has wandered? Are you more aware of how well others around you are managing their attention?

- Alternatively, if you did not engage in the Learning Practices to your satisfaction, write down what got in your way and your intentions to do better moving forward.
  - Don't beat yourself up. Practice self-compassion.
  - Decide if you want to give yourself more time to engage in the Learning Practices from Chapter 3 before moving forward with this chapter.

Self-Limiting Behaviors (SLBs)

One feature of Coach Your Self Up is for you to select a particular behavior that you would like to shift. In the spirit of improving your effectiveness at work, ideally you could choose something that is related to your work/career. Most self-limiting behaviors (SLBs) tend to affect several aspects of people's lives, whether they are conscious of it or not. Doing this work often helps individuals to see that their SLBs are more pervasive in their lives than they thought.

You will learn a standard approach and skills that will enable you to make sustainable behavior changes throughout your career. To gain some practical experience, you will start to apply those skills immediately to something you deem important to you right now.

Just what are Self-Limiting Behaviors (SLBs) anyway?

Most of us have heard somebody say, "If only she could get out of her own way." We may have experienced that one or more times ourselves: "If only I could get out of my own way."

The main idea is that something that a person is doing is barring her from being more successful than she is. An interesting point about these SLBs is that frequently the person is unaware that the SLB exists or is an issue.

Whether we are aware of it or not, we all get in our own way.

There is a useful tool that can provide a bit more context on this. It is called the Johari window. The Johari window was created in 1955 by two American psychologists, Joseph Luft (1916–2014) and Harrington Ingham (1914–1995), to help people better understand their relationship with self and others. The following image depicts this tool.

The Johari Window

	You Know	You Don't Know
Others Know	**Public**	**Blind Spot**
Others Don't Know	**Hidden**	**Unknown**

Public or Open: This quadrant represents things about a person that both she and her peers are aware of.

Hidden or Façade: This quadrant represents things about a person that she is aware of, but others are not.

Blind Spot: This quadrant represents information about a person that he is not aware of, but others are.

Unknown: This quadrant represents information about a person that he is not aware of, nor are others. One facet of interest in this area is our human potential. Our potential is unknown to us, and to others.

By now you may be thinking that you are aware of one or more SLBs that get in your way…or that you don't have any SLBs. Or maybe it is still unclear just exactly what an SLB looks like. Regardless of where you are on this, here is a list of some common examples of SLBs that apply to individuals in any role and at any organizational level, from individual contributors to senior-level leaders.

Examples of Common Self-Limiting Behaviors (SLBs):
- I frequently interrupt others when they're speaking
- I don't listen to others when they're speaking
- I succumb too easily to distractions (emails, text messages, etc.) when interacting with others
- I'm unable to say "no" (when it's a viable and reasonable option)
- I talk too much in meetings
- I don't speak up in meetings (even when something wants to be said)
- I speak too softly
- I solicit the input of others with no intention of changing my position
- I take credit for the work of others
- I blame others when things go wrong
- I talk about others behind their backs
- I react too negatively (or emotionally) when issues arise
- I get frustrated too easily, too often
- I complain a lot
- I'm unable / lack the confidence to make decisions
- I'm condescending to and/or dismissive of others
- I frequently bully others until they say that I am right
- I am consistently late
- I don't solicit advice or help from others even when it would be to my advantage to do so

While the prior list of examples applies to all of us, the following list is primarily applicable to individuals who are responsible for managing others.

Examples of Common Manager-Centric SLBs:

- I don't set clear expectations for one of more of my direct reports
- I don't conduct regular 1-on-1 meetings with one or more of my direct reports
- I frequently cancel 1-on-1 meetings with one or more of my direct reports
- I hold on to tasks/projects that could be effectively delegated
- I stay overly involved in the business of one or more of my direct reports (micro-managing)
- I avoid discussing performance concerns with one or more of my direct reports
- I don't provide ongoing feedback (positive and constructive) to one or more of my direct reports
- I discuss/raise/highlight performance concerns about one or more of my direct reports in a public setting
- I speak negatively or gossip about my boss or any other employees with one or more of my direct reports
- I hold on to strong performers when it might be in their best interest to move to another group or role
- I make decisions without soliciting appropriate team-member input
- I make promises/commitments I know my team can't deliver

Neither of these are exhaustive lists. Many more examples could be cited. Note that each of the SLBs listed is *behavioral* and not about skill. Certainly, there can be technical skill gaps (e.g., coding skills, analytical skills, financial skills, etc.) that also prevent a person from being more successful, but that is not the focus of Coach Your Self Up. We are focused on helping you make shifts in your behavioral patterns that affect how you show up.

Your Own Self-Limiting Behaviors (SLBs)

- Now it is your turn. Begin to identify some of your own SLBs that you would like to work on.
- Try to identify at least three. These could be straight off the prior lists of examples or any ideas those lists may have triggered for you.
- They should be observable behaviors.

SLB Selection Criteria:

- *Choose behaviors you WANT to change.* Behaviors you want to change for *yourself* that will help you be a better self. Do not choose things that you feel you *should* do for somebody else. If you don't really want to change, you won't.
- *Choose behaviors that occur at a high frequency.* As you begin to cultivate self-observation skills, it will be helpful to you to observe something that happens pretty often.
- *Choose behaviors that have a high personal impact.* If you have multiple behaviors you *want* to change that occur quite *often,* choose the one that you believe would have the biggest positive impact on you if you were able to make a shift.

Journaling

- Jot down your list of SLBs that you would potentially like to work on as you continue forward with Coach Your Self Up. If you can identify at least three, that's great.
- Don't worry if you are unable to come up with multiple SLBs, let alone one. We will address that shortly.

Back to the Johari Window

As we just saw, the Johari window is an excellent framework to think about how you see yourself vs. how others see you. It can also help support and accelerate your efforts to shift your SLBs.

You alone control the size of your public quadrant. There are two key tactics you can use to increase the size of your public quadrant to serve your ongoing professional and personal development.

1. *Seek Feedback*
   - The tactic of seeking feedback helps to expand your public quadrant horizontally by shrinking your blind spot quadrant. (See the graphic on the following page.) Seek feedback from others whom you trust and who observe you in action on a regular basis.
   - It would be normal for you to have one or more SLBs that you are unaware of. By proactively seeking feedback, you can increase your awareness of potential blind spots. As soon as you become aware of a blind spot, it moves into the public quadrant as it is no longer unknown to you.
   - Keep it simple. I encourage you to leverage the list of example SLBs. You can tell another person that you are working to improve yourself and want to identify areas to work on. Ask them if there is anything from that list that jumps out at them pertaining to your behavior.
   - Whether or not some of your opportunities for improvement are known to you, it will generally be helpful for you to periodically get input from others.

The Johari Window

Expanding Your Public Quadrant

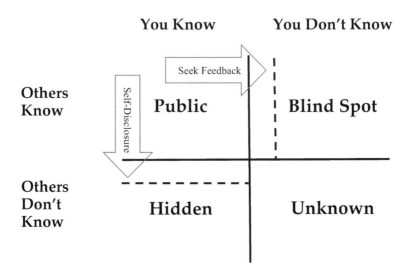

2. *Share with Others (Self-Disclosure)*
    *   This tactic expands your public quadrant vertically by reducing the size of your hidden quadrant.
    *   It can be super helpful to let others know what you are working on (i.e., which SLB you are trying to shift) so they can be supportive of your efforts. This is what I mean when I say, "The most effective self-coaching involves the support of others."
    *   For example, if you are working on becoming a better listener by interrupting others less often, it is easy to imagine how helpful it would be to have others who could provide you feedback on a timely basis (e.g., just after meetings or conversations).
    *   As with seeking feedback, you want to be discerning as to who you engage with. This is personal and puts you in a place of vulnerability. You do not need to share this information widely. Pick a person or two that you know is/are in a position to see you in action and whom you

trust to handle this in a professional and compassionate manner. (If you are comfortable sharing more broadly, power to you. For most people, however, sharing with a small number of confidantes is likely to be the most effective approach.)

Periodically revisit the Johari window and ask yourself, "Where would it serve me to solicit feedback from others?" and "Where would it serve me to disclose to others the focus of my current self-development efforts?"

1. Seek feedback to learn about your blind spots.

2. Disclose to others the focus of your development efforts to enlist their support.

Both of these tactics will help you significantly in your career.

SLBs – It's Time to Pick One

To get maximum value out of this book, choose one of your own SLBs to work on for the remainder of our journey together.

You might be inclined to work on more than one. Working on one behavior at a time makes it much more likely that you will experience a palpable shift. So, just choose one for now. You can always work on others in the future—and in fact that's a key point here—you are learning a repeatable process.

If you know which SLB you want to work on:
- Reflect on, and write about, the "better self" that shifting this behavior will help you become.

If you have a few potential SLBs to choose from but do not know which one to choose:
- Reflect on, and write about, how the selection criteria (page 64) align with the different SLBs you are considering.

If you have been *unable* to identify any SLBs to work on:
- Reflect on, and decide, how you will choose one soon—preferably within the next week.
- If needed, read the relevant sections ahead (either "SLBs - You Cannot Think of Any" or "SLBs – You Don't Want to Do This") for ideas.

SLBs – You Cannot Think of Any *(skip if not applicable)*

Some of you may be frustrated or uncomfortable that you cannot think of anything to work on. Don't worry, that's normal and ok.

As we just discussed with the Johari window, if you cannot think of something to work on, the best way to figure this out is to ask for feedback. If you are comfortable doing so, decide which person or persons (e.g., your boss, your teammates, your best friend, your partner, etc.) you would ask to give you feedback on any behaviors they see in you that, given the chance, they would encourage you to work on. Remember to consider using one or both lists of sample SLBs (pages 62 & 63) when asking for this feedback.

If soliciting feedback isn't feasible for any reason, as a "fall back" plan you might work on improving your attention. I have not met very many people who wouldn't benefit from improving their attention management skills.

Note: If you are uncomfortable with soliciting feedback, that in itself is a self-limiting behavior you will want to examine someday. It is likely not a great fit for an entrée into self-coaching as it may not occur frequently enough.

SLBs – You Don't Want to Do This *(skip if not applicable)*

Similarly, it is quite normal to have strong resistance to this type of work. Our egos do not like change and your ego is likely sending you lots of messages along the lines of, "We are just fine here, we don't need to be making any tough changes, life is hard enough without taking on this additional work."

So, if you find yourself resisting this, my experience is that there is often some significant SLB that you are already aware of that you know it would help you to work on, BUT it feels too big and/or too scary to tackle. If that idea resonates with you, I encourage you to go ahead and tackle that SLB (assuming it meets the selection criteria on page 64).

If there is not some obvious SLB you are resistant to tackle, and you are just resistant in general, you might work on improving your superpower of managing attention. This is an area where many of us succumb to poor behaviors.

Moving Forward

At this point you have either selected a specific SLB to work on or identified action steps for how you will select one soon. Well done!

To get maximum value out of this book, **choose one of your own SLBs to work on** for the remainder of our journey together.

CHAPTER 4 SUMMARY
Self-Limiting Behaviors (SLBs)

- Self-Limiting Behaviors (SLBs) block us from achieving our full potential.

- We may or may not be aware of our SLBs.

- The Johari window helps us think about how we see ourselves vs. how others see us.

- We can seek feedback from others to reduce our blind spots and potentially identify unknown SLBs.

- We can disclose to others the SLB we are working on to enlist their support.

- Working on one SLB at a time is the most effective approach.

- Working on one SLB for the remainder of this book provides hands-on experience with applying the self-coaching principles and skills.

Chapter 5

The Stories We Tell Ourselves

Introducing the Concept of Stories

Take a few moments to look at the picture and think about what you believe is *really* happening or has *really* just happened.

Spend a few minutes in your journal quickly answering the following four questions about the picture. This should take no more than one or a few sentences or bullet points for each question.

1. What is happening? Who are these people?
2. What has led up to this situation?
3. What is being thought? What is wanted? By whom?
4. What will happen next?

*****

Did you see the man as having the power here? Or maybe you saw the woman in power? Or maybe you saw them as peers?

Did you perceive that either the man or the woman was "in trouble" with the other?

Did you see this as a first encounter between these two discussing the topic at hand, or as a recurring scenario with maybe one or both parties reaching their wit's end?

Did you notice facial expressions?

Did you notice that it was relatively easy to answer the four questions once you got started? That's because we are story-generating creatures. Our brains are wired to make sense of the world, and generating stories is a key aspect of that.

Different people often come up with different answers to the four questions about the picture. This is because different people have constructed different stories about what they are seeing—even though they are seeing the exact same image.

This can be an "aha" moment for some when they realize how differently different people perceived the same image. Although this activity is contrived, it happens all the time in real life.

Here is a work-world example to consider. You and a few of your colleagues walk by a glass-walled conference room where the leadership team of your department is having a meeting. You all look at the group of people as you walk by. If I were to then ask each of you, "What do you think was going on in that meeting?" it is likely that you would all have slightly or very different responses, similar to the contrived example we just looked at with the picture.

The Ladder of Inference

This highlights one aspect of how that internal computer we have running 24/7 inside our heads shapes the way each of us views reality. Our different unique internal computers can, and often do, provide varying interpretations of the same observable data.

Our brains are wired to make sense of the world, and **generating stories** is a key aspect of that.

The Ladder of Inference is a **story-generating machine** and it is **always on.**

One formal name for this is the Ladder of Inference, first put forward by organizational psychologist Chris Argyris and used by Peter Senge in his book *The Fifth Discipline: The Art and Practice of the Learning Organization.*

The operation of the Ladder of Inference is something we want to bring more into the foreground, into our conscious awareness.

> Inference is the act or process of deriving logical conclusions from premises known *or assumed* to be true.

See the graphic on the following page for a visual representation of the Ladder of Inference.

Note that the first and last steps on this ladder (Observable "Data" and Experiences, and Actions) are darker than the steps in between. This is to denote that those steps take place *externally*. The steps in between take place *internally*, inside our brain/mind "computers."

We all start out with the same input—observable external "data" as a video camera would see it. After that our minds take over. We select "data" from what we observe. We add meaning and assumptions, to the data we selected, based upon our life experiences. We then infer conclusions and beliefs about the situation which drives our response (whether through action or inaction) in the external world.

I have mentioned that each of us has a unique internal "computer." Given that nobody else on the planet has had your *exact* life experiences, it stands to reason that nobody else on the planet will process observable data *exactly* as you would.

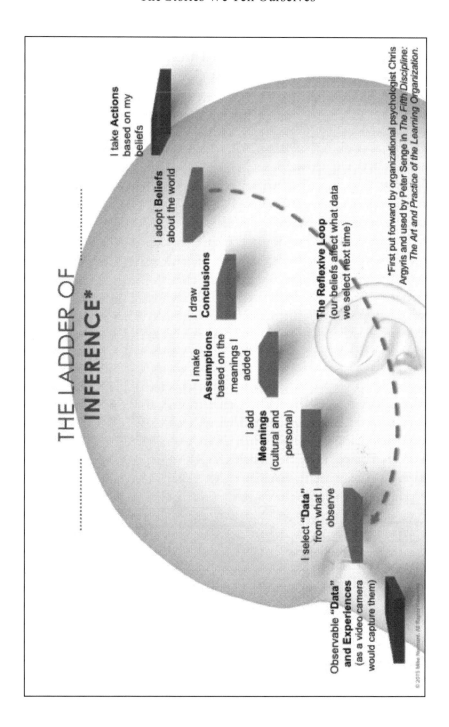

THE LADDER OF INFERENCE*

I take **Actions** based on my beliefs

I adopt **Beliefs** about the world

I draw **Conclusions**

I make **Assumptions** based on the meanings I added

I add **Meanings** (cultural and personal)

I select **"Data"** from what I observe

Observable **"Data" and Experiences** (as a video camera would capture them)

The Reflexive Loop (our beliefs affect what data we select next time)

*First put forward by organizational psychologist Chris Argyris and used by Peter Senge in *The Fifth Discipline: The Art and Practice of the Learning Organization*.

When we are taking in data from our surroundings, there is too much information coming at us to process it all. Our brains help us by being selective. In the prior graphic, you see the dotted line (symbolic of what is called The Reflexive Loop) that shows that our collective prior experiences influence how we will take in and process data in the future.

Let's go back to the work-world example where you and some colleagues walked by a glass-walled conference room where your department leadership team was meeting. Can you imagine that although each of you looks through the glass at the same time, you might be selecting different data to take in?

For example, you might each be focused on a different person sitting in that room. Or maybe two of you are focused on the same person, but one of you is focused on facial expressions while the other is focused on their posture. One of you might be more attuned to the perceived mood in the room by taking in a general sense of the body postures around the table.

You get the idea. We cannot take in all the data that is available, so we need to be selective. We are sophisticated in our selection, using our prior life experiences to help us know where to focus our attention, what data to select. And that is the data that we use to infer what is happening.

For our purposes, the important thing is to have general awareness that all of this is happening inside our head. Note that "Meanings," "Assumptions," "Conclusions," and "Beliefs" (the steps of the ladder) are all variations or flavors of what I refer to as "Stories."

In terms of the brain, some of these responses are building, over time, heavily reinforced neural pathways which lead to habitual or automatic responses on our part to certain stimuli. This is also an aspect of The Reflexive Loop. It saves us energy by reducing the amount of thinking activity we need to engage in.

Given that nobody else on the planet has had your *exact* life experiences, it stands to reason that **nobody else on the planet will process observable data *exactly* as you would**.

We move through the world:

- Taking in selected observable data through our filters, defined by our life experiences;
- Generating stories (meanings, assumptions, conclusions, beliefs) about the world, about ourselves, about others— about everything—based on that observable data and our prior life experiences;
- Acting (or not-acting) based upon those stories.

The Ladder of Inference is part of us and part of the way we process the world and create our reality. Just becoming aware that the Ladder of Inference is operational gives us the power to see it and know when it is affecting us.

More About "Stories"

You may have heard the joke about the two fish—where one fish asks the other as he swims by, "How's the water today, Sal?" And Sal stops and looks around and says, "What water?" Like water to a fish, stories are so omnipresent it's as if they were not even there.

> I propose that we are swimming in a sea of stories and that often times we are unaware of that.

A story is our interpretation of the facts. Stories serve as theories we use to help us explain *why*, *how*, and *what*.

Sometimes the word story throws people off. It is helpful to recognize that we are using the word story as a catchall phrase for things such as assumptions, conclusions, opinions, and beliefs.

Our stories feel like facts to us. We often believe that our stories are the Truth with a capital T. In fact, they are *our* truth, what I like to call "truth with a small t."

You will also find that often there are layers of story, and that poking a hole in one story reveals another underlying story...and so on.

Our stories feel like facts to us. We often believe that our stories are the Truth with a capital T. In fact, they are *our* **truth**— "truth with a small t."

Stories – A Few Simple Examples

There was an important team meeting held with ten participants. If the meeting had been recorded, the video would have shown that Jack did not say anything during the meeting.

Here are examples of stories created by Jack's silence:

- Team member 1 - "Jack didn't like what was being said."
- Team member 2 - "Jack was not engaged, and his mind was clearly elsewhere."
- Team member 3 - "I am pretty sure Jack wasn't prepared."

No doubt you can think of many other reasons why a person might not speak at a meeting.

Here is another example. Jill has not responded to an email. Here are a few different interpretations from Jill's colleagues:

- Colleague 1 - "Jill is mad at me about something."
- Colleague 2 - "She is avoiding me."
- Colleague 3 - "Jill does not care about my needs."

Again, I am sure you can think of other reasons why a person might not respond to an email.

These are simple but relevant examples of how stories get created. And they are everywhere.

As we just discussed, these stories are *our* truth and we often end up acting as if they were *the* Truth with a capital T.

We make assumptions and jump to conclusions multiple times a day—all variations of story.

These stories impact how we behave, how we show up.

Now that you have been thinking about which self-limiting behavior (SLB) you want to work on and have been introduced to the concept of stories, you are ready to jump into the next set of Learning Practices.

CHAPTER 5 SUMMARY

The Stories We Tell Ourselves

- Our brains are wired to make sense of the world, and generating stories is a key aspect of that.

- The Ladder of Inference is a helpful model that helps us understand how we generate stories.

- Nobody else shares our *exact* life experiences so it stands to reason that nobody else will see things *exactly* as we do.

- The Ladder of Inference is part of us and informs how we create our reality.

- Just being aware of the Ladder of Inference allows us to see when it is affecting us.

- Stories are our interpretations of the facts.

- Our stories feel like facts to us, like the Truth with a capital T. They are *our* truth, truth with a small t.

- We make assumptions and jump to conclusions multiple times a day—all variations of story.

- Our stories impact how we behave, how we show up.

Coach Your Self Up

Chapter 6
Learning Practices (Second Set)

Welcome to the second set of Learning Practices.

As with the first set of Learning Practices in Chapter 3, I would like you to take some time to step away from this book and engage with these practices. When I work with groups, we take two weeks. You may prefer a bit less or a bit more time.

Engaging in these practices helps to solidify key learning points and will provide you with insights that will more fully prepare you to take on the information in Chapter 7 and beyond.

These practices include opportunities for periodic reflection and journaling to help develop your self-observation skills. In an ideal world you would be able to engage in these practices every few days. *Consider scheduling a recurring 15-minute appointment with yourself to ensure this happens.*

Part I - Strengthening Attention

These practices help you continue to increase your ability to manage your attention. You are cultivating the superpower.

Bringing Yourself to the Present Moment for Five Minutes per Day

- This is a continuation of the practice from the first set of Learning Practices. See page 52 if you need a reminder.

Part II – Documenting Your Behavior Change Goal

There is power in writing down your goal statements. Dr. Gail Matthews, a psychology professor at Dominican University, ran a study in 2007 and found that people who wrote down their goals achieved their goals significantly more than those who did not write them down.

We will also leverage the Intentional Change Theory to create a more powerful version of your goal.

Part IIA – Writing down your Selected SLB

- You may have this written down already. If yes, jump ahead to Part IIB.
- If you know the SLB you will be working on and haven't written it down yet, please do so now. Then jump to Part IIB.
- If you have not selected your SLB yet, remember our goal is for you to select one soon. The sooner you can nail that down the better—as the self-observation practices ahead partially involve paying attention to your SLB.

Part IIB – Writing down a "Flipped" Aspirational Statement

Richard Boyatzis, a professor at Case Western Reserve University, published his work on the *Intentional Change Theory (ICT)* in 2006[7].

ICT research shows that a person is *much* more likely to sustain a personal change if it is in service of becoming their "ideal self"; that is some better version of their self that they aspire to be—as opposed to trying to "fix" something about their current self.

We will take advantage of the power of this research by creating an aspirational version of the behavioral shift we are trying to make.

We refer to the idea of a "flipped" statement in the context that we are "flipping" our SLB "upside-down" or "on its head" if you will. We are looking at it from a different, essentially "opposite" perspective. Instead of focusing on the old behavior we want to shift, we focus on the new behavior or state we aspire to.

> ICT research shows that a person is *much* more likely to sustain a personal change if it is **in service of becoming their "ideal self."**

---

[7] Richard E. Boyatzis and Kleio Akrivou, *The ideal self as the driver of intentional change* (Journal of Management Development, Vol. 25 No. 7, 2006. pp 624-642)

Your aspirational statement should be stated in a positive fashion and in the present tense, as if it were already happening.

- Examples:
    - o SLB 1 – "I frequently interrupt others."
    - o *Flipped Aspirational Statement 1 – "I am a great listener."*
        - ▪ Note: "I don't interrupt others" is not a positive statement as it refers to something you do *not* do as opposed to something you positively/proactively *do*. "I will be a great listener" is not as strong as it is not in the present tense.

    - o SLB 2 – "I say 'yes' to too many things."
    - o *Flipped Aspirational Statement 2 – "I am comfortable saying 'no' when it is a reasonable and viable option."*

Additional Examples - Aspirational Statements

When I teach this to a group, I find it is quite powerful to share the collective list of the participants' aspirational statements. Inevitably, at least one person mentions how helpful it was to see the group list and how that helped them to internalize the notion that, "I am not alone in having things to work on."

Many of us are working on improving ourselves. This is not anything to be embarrassed about or ashamed of. Regardless of whether you are working through this book on your own or with others, it will be helpful for you to see an actual list of aspirational statements from one of my groups. This may help you to recognize that you are not alone.

Of course, each of these corresponds to a self-limiting behavior that each person is trying to shift.

Many of us are working on improving ourselves. **You are not alone.**

Aspirational Statements
from a Coach Your Self Up Group

• I am comfortable saying "no" when it is a viable option.	• I am comfortable speaking up in meetings.
• I am comfortable saying "no" to items that are not main priorities.	• I am comfortable sharing my input in group discussions.
• I remain poised and calm even when things go wrong.	• I have great active listening skills.
• I am calm in stressful situations.	• I am comfortable asking others for what I need when I need it.
• I remain calm when I or my team is criticized.	• I appreciate when others recognize my efforts and thank me.

Part III – Cultivating Self-Observation Skills

We've talked about the importance of self-observation—it's the second step on the self-coaching path. The following practices help you to begin raising general awareness of (a) your selected self-limiting behavior (SLB) and (b) stories that are present in your life.

Part IIIA – Noticing Your Selected Self-Limiting Behavior (SLB)

Once you have identified the SLB you intend to work on, the next step is to begin to "notice" it. Here are suggested guidelines for this self-observation practice.

- **Periodically reflect** on how many times during the past several days you think/feel that you engaged in your selected SLB. Be honest with yourself.
- **Keep a record of your guesstimates in your journal.** Write down your thoughts on how much time elapsed between when the SLB took place and when you became aware of it. The more frequently and consistently that you invoke your self-observation practice, the shorter the elapsed time will become between engaging in your SLB and becoming aware of it.
- **We are not trying to change anything yet;** this is about using the power of your attention to bring your SLB more fully into your field of awareness, your conscious mind.

You are using the power of your attention to **bring your SLB more fully into your field of awareness.**

Part IIIB – Noticing Stories (Assumptions, Conclusions, Opinions, Beliefs)

- **Periodically reflect** on whether you see stories at play in your world. You might notice yourself making assumptions about situations or people and acting as if they were facts. Or you might notice others doing so.
- At this time, you are just beginning to recognize the presence of stories around you, whether they are your own or those of other people.

Journaling - Periodic Reflections (Parts IIIA and IIIB)

Every few days, reflect on and write about the following:
- Self-Limiting Behavior (SLB)
  - o Guesstimate – How many times did my SLB show up in the last few days?
  - o Roughly how much time elapsed between the occurrence of my SLB and my awareness that it happened?
- Stories
  - o What "stories" am I noticing in myself and others (e.g., assumptions, opinions, conclusions, beliefs)?

Something is Better than Nothing

Ideally, you will be able to commit to these Learning Practices. However, if you find yourself *not* doing anything because it feels like too much, then do less.

Doing something is always better than doing nothing.

You are just beginning to recognize the **presence of stories around you**, whether they are your own or those of other people.

Working with your Accountability Partner(s) (if applicable):

- Schedule a 30-minute conversation to take place during this Learning Practices time window.

Here is an optional discussion outline for this conversation:

- Spend a few minutes **"checking-in."** Confirm your intentions to pay attention to each other during this time.

- Focus your time talking about **where you are in relation to selecting and noticing your SLB.**
  - Have you selected one yet?
    - If yes, what is it? How have you framed it in aspirational language?
    - Have you started noticing it yet? Any insights?
    - If no, is there anything this group can do to help you move forward?

- Time permitting, discuss **anything interesting that has "come up" as you have been noticing stories.**

- **Determine if you want to do anything differently at your next Learning Practices meeting.** Each person briefly answers the following two questions:
  - What went well today that we want to continue?
  - What might we do next time to improve?

Summary of Learning Practices (Second Set)

- Part I – Strengthening Attention
  - Using your attention to bring yourself to the present moment for a total of at least five cumulative minutes per day

- Part II – Documenting Your Behavior Change Goal
  - Part IIA – Writing down the self-limiting behavior (SLB) you intend to work on
  - Part IIB – Leveraging the power of the Intentional Change Theory, writing down a "flipped" aspirational statement

- Part III – Cultivating Self-Observation Skills
  - Part IIIA – Becoming more aware of your SLB via periodic reflection and journaling
  - Part IIIB – Becoming more aware of the presence of stories (your own or those of others) in your life, via periodic reflection and journaling

---

Good luck with these Learning Practices. I hope you enjoy them. "See you" back here for Chapter 7 when you are ready.

"Being Here" Activity

Managing Attention – Focus on Your World

Sit up in your chair with both feet on the ground. You should be comfortable, but not slouched over. Take a few deep breaths.

With your eyes closed, breathe naturally and take just 30 seconds to focus your attention on what you are hearing (if you are hearing impaired improvise with one of your other senses).

What's the softest/quietest sound you can hear? Focus and hold your attention on that.

When you become distracted by a thought, a bodily sensation, or another one of your senses, just acknowledge the distraction, and gently let it go. Bring your attention back to the sound you are focused on.

Allow 30 seconds.

When you are ready, take one last deep breath and gently open your eyes and come back into your space.

Chapter 7

Speed Laddering and More

Welcome back.

Ideally, you have been "away" for a while, engaging in the Learning Practices from Chapter 6.

Before you dive in to this chapter, I invite you to take a minute and get a bit more *present* by engaging in the "Being Here" activity on the prior page. You will practice using your superpower of managing attention to focus on your world through one of your five senses. This will help to get you "here" mentally.

Journaling – Learning Practices - Reflection

Let's take a few minutes to reflect on your recent experiences.

- Write down a few sentences to capture your high-level thoughts and/or feelings about your experience with the Learning Practices and/or any other aspect of the work you have done so far with Coach Your Self Up.
- Alternatively, if you did not engage in the Learning Practices to your satisfaction, write down what got in your way and your intentions to do better moving forward.
  - o Don't beat yourself up. Practice self-compassion.
  - o Decide if you want to give yourself more time to engage in the Learning Practices from Chapter 6 before moving forward with Chapter 7.

The Ladder of Inference – A Story-Generating Machine
As noted earlier, the Ladder of Inference is a story-generating machine—and it is always on.

We make assumptions and jump to conclusions—all variations of story—multiple times a day. **These stories impact how we behave, how we show up.**

Activity – Speed Laddering

To make these ideas more tangible, there is an activity that I call Speed Laddering that I love to use when I am teaching a group.

I ask participants to pick somebody in the room that they don't know very well that has caught their attention for whatever reason (e.g., very quiet, talkative, jokes around a lot, asks lots of questions, wears interesting clothes, showed up late for today's workshop, anything!) and just spend 30 seconds reflecting on what other assumptions they have made about that person.

Since you are reading this chapter by yourself, you don't have a group of people around you to utilize for this activity. However, you are meeting new people all the time and / or seeing people as you are out and about living your life.

Think of somebody at work whom you have met or seen recently who caught your attention or triggered you in some way. (If nothing from your in-person experiences jumps to mind, think about people you see on TV. Politicians can be good fodder for this.) Go ahead and spend 30 seconds thinking about that person and what else you assume is likely to be true about her / him.

*****

What was that experience like for you? Were you able to articulate additional assumptions about the person you were thinking about?

The reason I include this activity is because of the profound effect it had on me when I was in the participant seat. During the first multiday session of the Hudson Institute of Coaching's coach certification program, we were led through this activity.

There I was, sitting in a large circle of 35 or so folks, most of whom I was just meeting for the first time. One person in the group had caught my attention due to his sense of humor. He had made multiple humorous comments that resulted in most of the people in the room literally laughing out loud.

Given 30 seconds to ponder what other assumptions I had about him, I was surprised what came out of me as I put pen to paper.

I believed it was important for him to be the center of attention. He used his humor to mask his lack of self-confidence and the fact that he was intimidated, maybe threatened, by being around so many other highly successful people.

I thought it was important for him to establish himself as the "funny guy" in this group before somebody else did (which by the way I was envious of as I often like to be the "funny guy" in a group).

The impact of this brief activity on me was borderline transformational. I had perceived myself as a person who was not judgmental of others. Period. (In hindsight, it is humorous to me that I thought this; but I did.) That 30-second activity ripped away the façade and revealed the judgmental human being that I am.

Going back to the Ladder of Inference, the observable data here was, "A person makes funny comments and people in the group laugh." From there I quickly had pegged this person as lacking confidence and being threatened. And for me that was real…that was *my* truth…and I saw it as *the* Truth. WOW. And to think I was doing this same thing with many of my colleagues at work, let alone with the other people in my life.

For me, this was a real "aha" moment where I became aware of how the Ladder of Inference was impacting me (mostly unconsciously) for large portions of my waking hours. Just becoming aware of that has helped me tremendously, as I am now much more conscious of how my Ladder of Inference operates. I am more able to catch myself generating stories.

Using the example above, I am now more likely to think, "Wait a minute, he just said some funny things (observable data), I have NO IDEA if he has confidence issues, so let that go and be open to learning more about him without that pre-judgment in place."

You too can be more cognizant of when your Ladder of Inference is operating and push the pause button to re-ground yourself. You can "climb down" your Ladder of Inference and remind yourself of what is observable data vs. what you have made up.

You too can be more cognizant of when your Ladder of Inference is operating and push the pause button to re-ground yourself. You can **climb down** your Ladder of Inference and remind yourself of what is observable data vs. what you have made up.

Activity – "You Have a New Manager"

Here's another activity that further illustrates our tendencies to generate stories.

New Manager #1

You have a new manager and you just had your first conversation with her. She told you that her style is very hands off. She'll assume all is going well and won't proactively reach out to you unless she believes there are concerns to address.

She's not a fan of regular one-on-one conversations but makes it clear that you are free to reach out to her anytime if you ever need her support.

Write down your responses to the three questions listed below.

Journaling

Imagine this is really happening to you—you have a new manager—and write down how you would respond to the following three questions:

1. What might my first impressions be of this new manager? What other thoughts come to mind about her/his management style?

2. What types of people do I think would want to work for this manager? Why?

3. What would I tell my colleagues at lunch who ask, "What's your sense of what it is going to be like working with your new manager?"

New Manager #2

You have a new manager and you just had your first conversation with him. He has recently worked for Amazon and he told you that one of the things that he appreciated about his experience there was that they encouraged vigorous debate amongst colleagues.

He acknowledged that you and your peers are super-smart people and that with this approach your good ideas can become great and your great ideas can become amazing.

Essentially, he will be working with all of you to help you get more comfortable challenging each other's ideas.

Write down your responses to the three questions listed on the prior page in regard to this second new manager.

Reflecting on Your Responses

Look at your responses for the New Manager #1 scenario, the hands-off manager. Consider the following common perspectives that I often hear:

- Excitement: "I'm excited to have a hands-off manager. I'm totally fine to be given lots of freedom and understand that if I make a mistake my manager should be on me for that."
- Anxiety: "I'm anxious about having a hands-off manager. I'm sure it will be just fine when things are going well, but when anything is even a slight bit off, I worry that she will jump down my throat with negative feedback. I'll be walking on eggshells trying not to make a mistake."
- Anger/Frustration: "I feel cheated. This manager is shirking one of the most important aspects of managing, which is to provide feedback and guidance to her employees. Frankly this sucks."

Do your responses fit into one of these perspectives? Of course, there are numerous other possible perspectives and none of them are right or wrong.

Let's move on and look at your responses for the New Manager #2 scenario, the manager who recently worked at Amazon. Consider the following common perspectives:

- This is bad: "I have read negative things about Amazon's culture and how they totally trash each other's ideas. We've got a good thing going with our team and the last thing we need is to start beating up each other's work."

- This is good: "This is a breath of fresh air. I have read great things about Amazon's culture and how they use the power of constructive debate to turn good ideas into great ideas. I am looking forward to injecting this energy into our team."

Do your responses fit into one of these perspectives? As with the prior scenario, there are numerous other possible perspectives and none of them are right or wrong.

Your Ladder of Inference Influences Your Responses

We typically find that our Ladders of Inference are hard at work (although none of this is hard, it all happens quite effortlessly) in interpreting these situations.

When I'm working with a group, I ask if anyone has ever worked for "that manager" before. For example, in scenario #1, I ask "How many of you have ever worked for a hands-off manager before?" Lots of hands go up.

When I ask if that prior experience influenced their responses to the three questions, the answer is always "yes!" This makes total sense. If you worked for a hands-off manager before, those life experiences logically inform your perception of this next hands-off manager.

You may notice that you will tell yourself (and others) that you *know* what this manager is like because you have *worked for her* before—even though this is a brand-new manager whom you have never met. I've heard some people talk about situations like this using the phrase, "I've seen this movie before."

You may notice that you will tell yourself (and others) that you *know* **what this manager is like because you have** *worked for her* **before**—even though this is a brand-new manager whom you have never met.

In the second scenario, there is another "loaded" piece of observable data in the mix. The new manager used to work at Amazon. On August 15, 2015, Amazon's culture was the subject of an article in the New York Times (NYT).

This article was the most commented-on, and one of the most-read, NYT articles of 2015. It was the catalyst for additional related NYT articles and some public sparring between Amazon and the NYT.

If you read any of those articles, or heard about them, depending on your perspective, you might have drawn a conclusion that their management practices were effective (good) or ineffective (bad).

Something that simple could influence your perception of a new manager who has joined your company from Amazon. (This applies to a manager coming from any prior employer about which you have some perception, positive or negative.)

If you have worked in an organization of any kind, you know managers come in all flavors—there are great managers and not-so-great managers inside most organizations. Yet in a situation like this your Ladder of Inference is inclined to lead you to believe this specific manager will be "good" or "bad" based upon what you have read or heard about Amazon's management reputation and your perception of whether it is positive or negative.

What Would the Video Camera Show?

When I am teaching a group, there are usually several "aha" moments associated with the Speed Laddering and "You Have a New Manager" activities. Individuals see how active their Ladder of Inference is and how much it influences their day-to-day experiences through the generation of stories.

We mentioned that it is helpful for you to "climb back down" your Ladder of Inference when you recognize you might be generating stories. One way to do this is to ask yourself, "What would the video camera show?"

For the New Manager #1 scenario, all that the video camera would show is that she told you she has a hands-off style and that you are free to reach out to her anytime for her support.

Recognizing that, it would occur to you that anything else you have come up with about the manager is some flavor of story.

I hope you are feeling more comfortable with the idea of the stories we tell ourselves and are starting to recognize them more readily.

CHAPTER 7 SUMMARY
Speed Laddering and More

- The Speed Laddering activity highlights how fast we can climb our Ladder of Inference and make judgments about people and things. It can happen in a flash.

- The "You Have a New Manager" activity highlights how much our prior experiences influence our judgements. We say things like "I've seen this movie before," even when it's really a new movie.

- When we recognize that we are dealing with stories, we can climb down our Ladder of Inference to consider what is observable data vs. what we have made up.

- One technique for climbing down our Ladder of Inference is to ask ourselves, "What would the video camera show?"

Five Challenging Questions:

1. How do you know that to (always) be true, *<your first name>?*

2. What other valid stories could one create based upon the same observable data?

3. How might you act differently, *<your first name>,* if you didn't believe that story to be true?

4. Do you think it would serve you to act that way, *<your first name>?*

5. How will you experiment with acting differently, *<your first name>?*

Chapter 8

Challenging Your Stories

Being Response-Able

Let's move into the third step of the self-coaching path—Being Response-Able. We have noted that coaches ask their clients challenging questions. A key aspect of self-coaching is learning to *ask yourself* challenging questions.

Before we discuss the list of *five challenging questions*, here is some interesting research on self-talk.

> **Self-Talk – The Power of Using Your Given Name**
>
> (Brief excerpts from "The Voice of Reason," in *Psychology Today*, June 2015)
>
> In a series of groundbreaking experiments, Ethan Kross, Ph.D., Professor of Psychology at the University of Michigan, has found that how people conduct their inner monologues has an enormous effect on their success in life. Talk to yourself with the pronoun I, for instance, and you're likely to fluster and perform poorly in stressful circumstances. Address yourself by your name and your chances of acing a host of tasks, from speech making to self-advocacy, suddenly soar.
>
> "When dealing with strong emotions, taking a step back and becoming a detached observer can help," Kross explains. "It's very easy for people to advise their friends, yet when it comes to themselves, they have trouble. But people engaging in this

process, using their own first name, are distancing themselves from the self, right in the moment, and that helps them perform."

The findings are applicable to the entire range of social relationships, Kross contends, because asymmetry pervades the way people think about all problems—better at dealing with others' than with their own. Self-distancing, he believes, can bring clarity in thinking about social conflicts, whether in business or romance.

Most of the people I work with resonate with the idea that it seems easier to advise their friends than themselves.

The simple act of **addressing yourself in the third person** shifts something in the brain, which makes it more likely that you can get "outside" of yourself and be more objective.

Challenging Your Stories

As we become more aware of our stories, that awareness opens the door for us to begin challenging them.

The objective is to evaluate just how "truthful" our stories are. By stepping back and looking at them from different angles, more objectively, we often find that they are not the Truth (with a capital T) that we assumed them to be. This opens the door for experimenting with acting differently.

Here are *five challenging questions* you can use in all situations.

> Five challenging questions:
>
> 1. How do you know that to (always) be true, *<your first name>*?
>
> 2. What other valid stories could one create based upon the same observable data?
>
> 3. How might you act differently, *<your first name>*, if you didn't believe that story to be true?
>
> 4. Do you think it would serve you to act that way, *<your first name>*?
>
> 5. How will you experiment with acting differently, *<your first name>*?

The reference in these questions to *<your first name>* is leveraging what we just read about the power of talking to yourself using your given name.

For question #1, you see that the word *always* is in parentheses. We will address this when we look at deep stories.

For question #2, the goal is NOT to create a laundry list of alternatives but to think of at least one or two. Just knowing there are other possible stories loosens your brain's grip on *your* story being the Truth (capital T).

You may have noticed that question #4 is a closed question (i.e., it can only be answered with a "yes" or a "no"). This is a simple question that should always be answered with a strong "yes." This taps into the Intentional Change Theory that we are more likely to make a change if we believe it helps us to become a version of ourselves that we aspire to be. Saying "yes" to question #4 confirms that acting differently can help you on your path to becoming a more successful you.

In question #5, the word experiment is important. If you think about a scientist conducting an experiment, there is never a failure. Although the outcome may not be what was intended or hoped for, the experiment reveals data/information/an outcome. That is the main intent of an experiment.

For many stories, especially like the simple ones we have discussed so far, acting differently will often be binary (e.g., instead of avoiding doing something, I will choose to do it).

If we treat our attempts at acting differently as experiments, that can make it easier to go for it and to review the outcome with a neutral, nonjudgmental stance.

Finally, you will note that question #5 is phrased so that the answer will be an action to propel you forward.

We challenge our stories to **evaluate how "truthful" they are.**

Challenging Our Stories – An Example

Earlier we introduced a simple example where individuals were making up stories as to why somebody (we called her Jill) was not responding to her emails (page 82). Let's assume Jack is one of those individuals. Let's walk through an example of how Jack could use these *five challenging questions* to challenge his belief that Jill is mad at him.

Since Jack has been through Coach Your Self Up, he has learned to become better at detecting when stories are present and potentially getting in his way. He is aware that his progress on some projects is hindered due to his current situation with Jill. He decides to pull out the list of challenging questions and see if they might help him in this situation.

Jack's story – "Jill is mad at me." (Note that in the example below, the statements within the quotation marks represent Jack's self-talk.)

Question #1 - "How do you know that to (always) be true, Jack?"

- In this instance, the word "always" is not relevant.
- Path 1 – Jack chuckles to himself because he realizes he has no idea if Jill is actually mad at him. He recognizes this is a story he made up. "I guess I don't really know that to be true." (Jack can skip to question #3.)
- Path 2 – Jack has had prior experiences that are informing his belief that Jill is mad at him. He is pretty sure this is true. "In the past, when Jill did not respond to some of my other emails, it turned out that she was mad at me."

Question #2 (if needed) - "What other valid stories could one create based upon the same observable data?" (The observable data in this situation is that Jill did not respond to Jack's email.)

- "Sure, there are lots of reasons why she may not be responding to my emails. She might be super busy with other priorities. She might be fighting one or more fires. Maybe something difficult is going on in her personal life. Hmm. I guess I cannot really be certain she is mad at me."
- Jack's brain is loosening its grip on his story about her being

mad at him.

Question #3 - "How might you act differently, Jack, if you didn't believe this story to be true?"

- "If I did not believe Jill was mad at me I would do a few things differently. First, I would not be trying to avoid her in general. Second, I would be more proactive in getting her input, either by resending those emails and/or stopping by her desk."

Question #4 – "Do you think it would serve you to act that way, Jack?"

- "YES! I need her input to move forward."

Question #5 – "How will you experiment with acting differently, Jack?"

- "I will just do it. I will stop avoiding Jill. If I see her, I will stop her and ask her about it. And I will resend the email. Maybe I will preface it with a sentence asking if she has the time to get to this in the next few days or if not, what quick advice might she be able to give me to push this forward."

Question #5 is phrased such that the answer will always be an **action to propel you forward**.

Reflecting on the Example

I hope you can see how powerful the *five challenging questions* can be. You can imagine the conversation Jack had with himself in his head only took a few minutes. Of course, it is not always this easy—but often it is!

Let's look at the initial situation from a more distanced viewpoint. If you asked Jack why he was stuck, he would be very likely to say something like, "It is pretty hard to make any progress when Jill is mad at me." A savvy observer would note, "Actually, Jack is not making progress because he *thinks* Jill is mad at him. The issue here is not with Jill, it is with the story Jack is telling himself about Jill."

What if the story is True (capital T)?

A question that often comes up is, "What if my story turns out to be True (with a capital T)? Wouldn't that mean I was right all along and hence wasted energy and time with this process of asking the challenging questions?"

This is a great question and one that could deter some of you from challenging your stories. We noted that the objective of doing this is to try and step back and evaluate just how "truthful" our stories are. Your story could turn out to be True.

Even if you determine that to be the case, it will still have been extremely valuable for you to have challenged your story.

When you challenge a story and find that it is NOT the Truth (more frequent), you clear a path to move forward on something where your story was blocking you. In our example, if Jack found that Jill was not mad at him, he could stop avoiding her and get on with reaching out to her for what he needs.

When you challenge a story and find that it is True (less frequent), you now need to deal with that confirmed reality. If Jack found that Jill was actually mad at him, he could then decide if he wanted to continue to avoid Jill (likely not so productive) or determine what actions he could take to address Jill's frustrations.

Regardless of whether you find that your story is simply *your* truth, or is in fact a more objective Truth, having that clarity provides you with important information regarding appropriate next steps you might take.

Tying Back to the Ladder of Inference

Let's look at how this all connects back to the Ladder of Inference.

We know this story-generating machine (the Ladder of Inference) is running all the time. The more we reinforce our reflexive/habitual patterns, the stronger those specific neural pathways become. This impacts the "data" we select when processing observable data in the future (as denoted by the lighter dotted line, the Reflexive Loop, in the image on the next page).

The idea of identifying and challenging our stories is about using our attention and awareness at the top of the ladder—JUST prior to taking an action.

When we can see that our typical response is based upon one or more of our stories, we can *challenge* our stories and consider making a different (non-habitual, more aware) response. We can envision new possibilities. This is denoted by the darker dotted line, the Conscious Loop, in that same image.

Ultimately, by experimenting with new responses, we begin to change our filters. The power of our Reflexive Loop will diminish (as denoted by the large "X" in the image), and our Conscious Loop will strengthen. This ties directly back to the concept of neuroplasticity and creating new neural pathways in the brain. We are becoming more response-able.

Note that any new responses will feel unnatural at first, like putting on somebody else's clothes. You are forcing the brain to take a neural path that is less traveled (or maybe has never been traveled). It is important to stick with it, even though it feels awkward or clumsy; it takes practice!

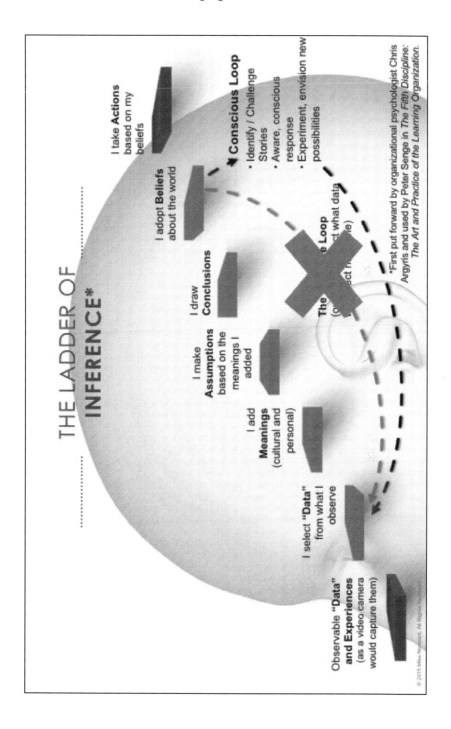

THE LADDER OF INFERENCE*

I take **Actions** based on my beliefs

I adopt **Beliefs** about the world

I draw **Conclusions**

I make **Assumptions** based on the meanings I added

I add **Meanings** (cultural and personal)

I select **"Data"** from what I observe

Observable **"Data" and Experiences** (as a video camera would capture them)

Conscious Loop
• Identify / Challenge Stories
• Aware, conscious response
• Experiment, envision new possibilities

The ___ **Loop**

*First put forward by organizational psychologist Chris Argyris and used by Peter Senge in *The Fifth Discipline: The Art and Practice of the Learning Organization.*

By experimenting with new responses, we begin to change our filters. The power of our Reflexive Loop will diminish, and our Conscious Loop will strengthen. We are creating new neural pathways in the brain. **We are becoming more response-able.**

CHAPTER 8 SUMMARY

Challenging Your Stories

- For effective self-talk, addressing ourselves by our first name allows us to get "outside" of ourselves and be more objective.

- As we become more aware of our stories, that opens the door for us to challenge them.

- The objective of challenging our stories is to assess how truthful they are.

- There are *five challenging questions* we can use in all situations.

- The *five challenging questions* lead us to action—to experimenting with acting differently.

- Experimenting with new behaviors builds new neural pathways and diminishes the power of our Ladder of Inference's Reflexive Loop, strengthening our Conscious Loop.

- This approach helps us become more response-able.

Chapter 9

Deep Stories

I have mentioned that you will often find there are layers of story, so that poking a hole in one story reveals another underlying story, and so on. Along those lines, I would like to introduce you to the concept of what I call "deep" stories. (These may also be referred to as self-limiting beliefs.)

> Deep stories are powerful and pertain to how we view ourselves and/or how we view our world.

Here are a few examples:
- "I am not a risk taker."
- "I'm always right."
- "I'm not smart enough."
- "Conflict is bad."
- "The world is an unfriendly place."

While all of our stories feel like the Truth (capital T), these deeper stories are usually years, decades or even a lifetime in the making. They are more ingrained and hence feel much more like they really are the (capital T) Truth.

It is totally normal and ok to be highly skeptical of this notion when you are first exposed to it. I remember when I told somebody, "I am not a risk taker," and she told me that was a story. I was incensed and incredulous. I thought to myself, "I know myself. Who is this person (whom I have just met) to tell me that this isn't true? I am not a risk taker. Period. End of story. Fact."

Now, given that this information was being shared with me in a kind and supportive way, and it was within the context of a personal growth workshop, I recognized my strong resistance. I worked hard to be open to the possibility that this "fact" about me (that I was not a risk taker) might be a story. But I had lots of internal resistance—I assume you will as well.

While all of our stories feel like the Truth (capital T), these deeper stories are usually **years, decades or even a lifetime in the making**. They are more ingrained and hence feel much more like they really are the (capital T) Truth.

Look back at the short list of sample deep stories. Assuming that they are stories, can you think of how they could be self-limiting to a person?

Here are a few examples:

- "I am not a risk taker" could cause a person to consistently play it safe and shy away from trying more innovative or creative solutions that might have a more positive impact on the business.

- "I'm always right" could lead to a person having strained relationships at work. If colleagues know that ultimately this person will have their way, it's likely they will disengage and stop bringing their own good ideas to the table.

- "I'm not smart enough." A person with this story might pass up all sorts of interesting opportunities at work due to his fear of being found out as being less smart than people think he is. (This is a common story: "I'm not <blank> enough.")

- "Conflict is bad" could lead to a person being overly conflict avoidant and/or being judgmental of people who value conflict as "bad" people. (Note that this and the following deep story are about one's view of the world, something outside of the self. The prior examples are about the self.)

- "The world is an unfriendly place" could lead a person to put her energies into protecting herself from others as opposed to helping them.

Activity – Some of Your Own Deep Stories

Following is a long list of common deep stories.

- Read this list and see if any of them resonate with you and/or trigger other ideas.

- Capture your thoughts. You might mark up the list in some way or take notes in your journal.

- This is not easy. Remember it is common to experience resistance to the idea that these might be stories because they absolutely feel like facts. I am not asking you to believe this at this point, I am asking you to be curious and open-minded to the possibility that these are stories.

- Some of you may find one or many items that you quickly relate to while some of you may find none. Both are normal.
- It is more important that you walk away from this with awareness about the notion of deep stories rather than having identified one or more of your own. That said, take this opportunity to think seriously about this for yourself.

Be curious and open-minded to the **possibility** that these are stories.

Deep Stories - Examples

- I need perfection
- I'm not _____ enough ("good," "smart," "educated," "rich," "successful," "happy," etc.)
- I'm fundamentally flawed in _____
- I can't be happy until _____
- If I "show up" the way I really am, people will (judge me (harshly), reject me)
- I need to be liked by everybody I work with
- It's important that others see me as successful
- I'm responsible for the happiness of others
- Other people are responsible for my happiness
- I don't have time to take care of myself
- I'm not a risk taker
- Conflict is bad (or conflict is good)
- I need harmony in my environment
- I need others to see me as "strong"

- I believe that showing vulnerability is a sign of weakness
- I'm smarter than everybody else
- I'm always right (or I'm never right)
- I can't win (or I can't lose)
- I have to prove myself every day
- Things will always go wrong
- It's always my fault when things go wrong
- I'm supposed to fail/I'm not supposed to succeed
- I need certainty
- I need security
- I need to be in control
- I can't interact socially
- I'm not supposed to outshine certain people in my life
- I need to gain approval from _____ (my parents, my partner, my friends, etc.)
- I need to get angry with people in order to ensure they get the message
- I need everyone to agree with the solution in order for it to be successful
- I need to be happy; life's too short for anything else
- People don't listen to me
- There's not enough opportunity for all of us to be successful
- I need to have intellectual mastery in one or more areas
- I can't handle rejection/isolation
- I can't express my emotions
- I need to express my intense emotions
- I'm not creative
- My past defines me; I will never overcome it
- It's too late to change
- I can't _____ (because I'm not wired that way)
- I never _____ (because I'm not wired that way)
- I often beat myself up about _____

- Once you have completed reviewing the list and capturing your notes, see if you can hypothesize if one or more potential deep stories might contribute to the self-limiting behavior (SLB) that you are working on.
- For example, let's say a person has an SLB of not speaking up in meetings. You can see how that person might have an underlying deep story of "I'm not smart enough," or "If I say what I really feel people will judge me," or something else.
- Capture your thoughts on this in writing.

Personal experiences with this activity vary widely. On one end of the spectrum a person may be entrenched in their view that these are facts, not stories. At the other end of the spectrum an individual is beyond excited to think that s/he could potentially shift one or more of these stories about themselves.

Where are you on that spectrum at this moment?

In her book, *DROP IT: A coach's secret to productivity, presence and possibility*, Linda Newlin shares a Rwandan proverb—

"You can outrun what runs after you. You can't outrun what runs inside of you."

Stories, most notably deep stories, "run inside of you."

Linda's book has additional guidance and tools to help you identify, explore and drop your deep stories and self-limiting beliefs.

Tying Back to the Self-Coaching Path

Let's look at how this all fits into the self-coaching path. (There is a larger version of this graphic on page 24.)

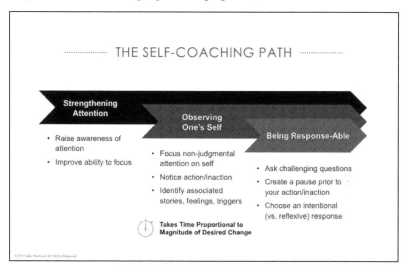

In step 2, Observing One's Self, we pay attention to our self-limiting behavior (SLB). As we get more attuned to our SLB, we use our self-observation skills to look for and identify any stories, as well as any feelings (e.g., anger, sadness, joy) or triggers associated with our SLB. This is the goal of self-observation.

It is common to find **one or more deep stories that underlie our SLBs**.

For example, as I pay attention to my SLB of "not being able to say 'no'," I may uncover a deep story that "I need everyone to like me." Accepting that as a story about myself, or at least being open to the possibility that it is a story, is a prerequisite to being able to start challenging it. (We know this is difficult...IT FEELS LIKE THE TRUTH.) But I will need to work through that story if I want any chance of creating a sustainable shift around my SLB of not being able to say "no."

Once we believe we have identified our underlying story or stories, we can shift to the third step on the self-coaching path; Being Response-Able. This is where we start to challenge those stories and experiment with new ways of responding or acting. This is where we begin to make more aware choices in the moment.

Let's look through another conceptual lens at this process of shifting an SLB.

Typical Evolution of Shifting a Self-Limiting Behavior (SLB)

As you have experienced with the Learning Practices, I encourage you to reflect on your selected SLB a few times per week. In the beginning, you might not "notice" that your SLB occurred until several days later when you pause to reflect.

- Example – During a moment of reflection on your SLB of interrupting others, you realize that you interrupted people in multiple situations earlier today. You weren't really aware of that until this moment of self-reflection.

As you continue to practice self-observation, **the amount of time** between the occurrence of your SLB and your awareness of it **will shrink**.

Your brain has been alerted: "Oh, you are interested in this behavior...I'll bring it to your attention sooner." As the elapsed time shrinks, you can start to also observe and reflect upon stories and feelings associated with the SLB.

- Example – As your brain starts paying more attention to your SLB of interrupting others, you might realize *just after a meeting* that you interrupted multiple times. Reflecting on that, you might recognize that you were feeling impatient and had a story that "other people weren't understanding my point-of-view (POV) and I needed to interrupt in order to get them to understand." You start to challenge that story, using the *five challenging questions*.

With continued self-observation, you will start being aware of your SLB *while you are experiencing it*—as well as noticing your associated stories and feelings in real-time.

- Example - Eventually you will catch yourself in the moment you are interrupting somebody. You could say, "I'm sorry I just interrupted you, please continue." After the meeting you affirm with yourself that you were (again) feeling impatient in that moment. You also experienced that after the other person finished their thought, you were still able to convey your POV. You realize you did not need to interrupt in order to accomplish this (which was your story).

For many SLBs, you will eventually notice your trigger(s) **prior to the SLB occurring** such that you are able to make an intentional choice (i.e., be response-able) before the behavior arises and preempt your SLB altogether.

- Example - You catch yourself being triggered (feeling impatient) and are ready to interrupt when you bite your tongue and pay closer attention to the speaker in service of your *aspiration* to be a better listener. You will ensure your POV is heard. And it is possible your POV may be modified based upon having attentively listened to the other person.

One other important piece of self-observation that we have not really touched on yet has to do with "triggers." In general, a trigger is some common "thing" that occurs just prior to engaging in your SLB. We will look at additional information about triggers in the upcoming Learning Practices.

Speaking of which, we are ready to jump into the next set of Learning Practices. Let's go!

CHAPTER 9 SUMMARY

Deep Stories

- Deep stories are powerful and pertain to how we view ourselves and/or how we view our world.

- Deep stories can be profoundly self-limiting and hold us back from being more successful at work (and in all other facets of our lives).

- Deep stories are often years, decades, or even a lifetime in the making. They really feel like the Truth (with a capital T).

- It's ok, even expected, to be highly skeptical of this notion. Therefore, I encourage you to be curious and open-minded to the possibility that these are stories, not facts.

- It is common to find one or more deep stories that underlie our SLBs.

- As we continue to practice self-observation, the amount of time between the occurrence of our SLB and our awareness of it will shrink.

- As our awareness of our SLB heightens, we can look for underlying stories and triggers.

Chapter 10

Learning Practices (Third Set)

Welcome to the third and final set of Learning Practices.

I hope you have experienced the value of the prior two sets of Learning Practices and will take some time to step away from this book to engage in this third set. I suggest two weeks; you may prefer more or less time.

Engaging in these practices allows you to continue to heighten your awareness of your self-limiting behavior and stories while forming new habits (and new neural pathways) around self-observation.

As with the first two sets of Learning Practices, there are opportunities here for periodic reflection and journaling. Use your experience with the prior Learning Practices to inform how you will encourage yourself to do this work during this time window.

Strengthening Attention

There are no assigned Learning Practices solely pertaining to strengthening your attention. Given the importance of this superpower, I encourage you to continue to regularly practice bringing your attention to the present moment—"being present."

This is a **lifelong practice**. Keep working on your superpower of managing attention in whatever manner best serves you.

Part I – Additional Information on Triggers

In Part III of these Learning Practices, you will begin to look for triggers associated with your selected self-limiting behavior (SLB). To prepare for that, here is some helpful information about triggers.

Common Types of Triggers

At the end of Chapter 9, we noted that for our purposes a trigger is some common feeling or situation that occurs just prior to engaging in your SLB.

We will use the same geography (Body, World, Mind) that we introduced for our attention to describe common types of triggers.

Body – some triggers are a *felt sensation* in the body. Examples:
- Shortness of breath
- Sweaty palms
- Tingling feeling somewhere
- A "pit" (tightening / clenching) in the stomach
- Feeling emotions (anger, happiness, sadness, etc.)

World – some triggers are *in our environment*. Examples:
- A particular person (this is one of the most common triggers)
- A particular sight / sound / smell
- A particular time of day
- A particular situation (e.g., attending meetings, giving presentations, and so forth)

Mind – some triggers occur *in our heads*. Examples:
- Thoughts about prior situations similar to the current one
- The tendency to label things as good vs. bad, right vs. wrong
- Thinking about emotions (anger, happiness, sadness). Some people "feel" their emotions in their bodies. Others may not be in touch with how their sadness "feels" in their body, but they know intellectually, "I feel sad."

Triggers come in all shapes and sizes, and **each of us is triggered by different things**.

Triggers are **goldmines** to work with as we seek to shift our behaviors.

Part II – Additional Information about Identifying and Challenging Stories

In Parts III and IV of these Learning Practices, you will be working with your stories. Some of those will be in relation to your selected self-limiting behavior (SLB) and some of them will be stand-alone.

Given where we are with this work, the following points can be helpful as you prepare for these practices.

Identifying Stories

The first step is seeing/recognizing/identifying a story; being able to accept that a story does (or even may) exist.

Once you identify the story you are then ready to challenge it, using the *five challenging questions* that we have introduced.

Trust that your instincts will be good at discerning between whether the story you are working with is deep or not.

Challenging Stories

For most of the stories you identify, you now have the knowledge and tools and are fully capable of challenging them and experimenting with acting differently.

In most cases the experimental response will simply be the opposite of your current response. For example, "I am not reaching out to Jill because I think she is mad at me—and now I will reach out to her," or "I am not proactively seeking feedback from my manager because she told me she is not a big fan of regular one-on-ones (which I assumed meant that she does not like to give feedback)—and now I will proactively seek feedback from her."

With a deep story, it is likely that it will take more time, maybe much more time, to even allow for the possibility it is a story. It will be helpful to delay "challenging" your deep stories until you have observed them for a while and gotten more comfortable with the idea that they are stories.

At this point, I encourage you to take more time to reflect on possible deep stories and push yourself to be open to the idea some of these things you believe to be facts about yourself are in fact a belief—a type of story.

Once you are confident that you have identified a deep story and accepted it as such and feel like you are ready to challenge it and experiment with acting differently, then go for it. Be patient with yourself on this. We will look at this topic in detail in Chapter 11.

Part III – Cultivating Self-Observation Skills (emphasis on your selected Self-Limiting Behavior (SLB) and associated stories, feelings, and triggers)

These practices help you to (a) continue raising general awareness of your selected self-limiting behavior (SLB) and (b) begin looking for any associated stories, feelings, and triggers.

You are still not trying to change anything yet; this exercise is about raising your awareness of your SLB and using the power of your attention to bring the pattern more fully into your field of awareness, your conscious mind.

Notice the action (or inaction)

- This is a continuation of the practice from the second set of Learning Practices. See page 90 (Part IIIA) if you need a reminder of the details.
- **Periodically reflect on**:
  - How many times you recently engaged in your SLB;
  - How much time elapsed between the occurrence of your SLB and your awareness of it.

In addition, notice and reflect on the stories, feelings and/or triggers (physical, mental, emotional) associated with your SLB.

Acknowledge that this can also be very difficult and potentially frustrating. Don't give up. Keep at it.

Part IV – Cultivating Self-Observation Skills (emphasis on Stories) and Being Response-Able Skills (emphasis on Challenging Stories)

These practices help you to (a) continue raising general awareness of stories and (b) begin challenging your stories and experimenting with acting differently. For ease of reference, the *five challenging questions* are repeated on the following page.

- As with the prior set of Learning Practices, **periodically reflect** on where you see stories at play in your life.
- **Challenge at least one (non-deep) story** and push yourself to **take action and experiment with acting differently**.

Push yourself to **take action and experiment with acting differently** at least once during this Learning Practices time window.

Five challenging questions:

1. How do you know that to (always) be true, *<your first name>?*

2. What other valid stories could one create based upon the same observable data?

3. How might you act differently, *<your first name>*, if you didn't believe that story to be true?

4. Do you think it would serve you to act that way, *<your first name>?*

5. How will you experiment with acting differently, *<your first name>?*

Journaling - Periodic Reflections (Parts III and IV)

Reflect on and write about the following:

- SLB:
  - Guesstimate – How many times did my SLB show up recently?
  - Roughly how much time elapsed between the SLB itself and my awareness that it happened?
  - What stories, feelings, and/or triggers have I noticed with my SLB?
- Stories
  - What stories am I noticing in myself and others?
  - Which one or more of those identified stories will I challenge and experiment with acting differently? (Remember to do this at least once.)

After using the *five challenging questions* on a story, write down how you will experiment with acting differently.

When you experiment with acting differently, write down what that experience was like.

Something is Better than Nothing

Ideally, you will be able to commit to the Learning Practices described in this chapter. However, if you find yourself NOT doing anything because it feels like too much, then do less.

Doing something is always better than doing nothing.

Working with your Accountability Partner(s) (if applicable):

- Schedule a 30-minute conversation to take place during this Learning Practices time window.

If you like, here is a recommended discussion outline:

- Spend a few minutes **"checking-in."** Confirm your intentions to pay attention to each other during this time.
- Focus your time on the following topics:
  - **Noticing your selected SLB:**
    - Is the amount of elapsed time shrinking between engaging in your SLB, and your awareness of it?
    - What associated stories, feelings and/or triggers are you noticing?
  - Did you **challenge a story and experiment with acting differently?**
    - If yes, how did that go?
    - If no, what is your plan for doing so soon?
- Time permitting, you can discuss **anything interesting that has come up for you as you have been doing this work.**
- This is the last of the suggested accountability partner meetings. It is up to you and your partner(s) to decide whether you want to schedule any future meetings to focus on your continued personal growth.

Summary of Learning Practices (Third Set)

- Parts I & II – Reading Additional Information
  - Triggers
  - Identifying and challenging stories

- Part III – Cultivating Self-Observation Skills (emphasis on your self-limiting behavior (SLB)
  - Becoming more aware of your SLB and related stories, feelings, and triggers via reflection and journaling

- Part IV – Cultivating Self-Observation Skills (emphasis on stories) and Being Response-Able Skills (emphasis on Challenging Stories)
  - Becoming more aware of stories via periodic reflection and journaling
  - Challenging at least one non-deep story and experimenting with acting differently

Good luck with these Learning Practices. I hope you enjoy them. "See you" back here for Chapter 11 when you are ready.

Chapter 11

Challenging Deep Stories –
Examples and Tactics

Welcome back.

Ideally, you have been "away" for a while engaging in the Learning Practices described in Chapter 10.

One of these statements describes where you are with challenging your stories:

- You have challenged one or more of your stories and successfully experimented with acting differently.
- You have challenged one or more of your stories and have identified how you would like to experiment with acting differently but have not done so yet.
- You have not yet challenged one of your stories.

It is important to meet yourself where you are. This is not a race and it is not about being right or wrong. If you are seeing stories and starting to challenge them and shift your actions, that is great.

If you are struggling to see stories at this point, that is also fine. Don't beat yourself up. Keep your eyes and ears open for situations where you or others are treating assumptions like facts. This is the clearest path to seeing stories in action.

Challenging Your Deep Stories – Differences in Using the *Five Challenging Questions*

This section describes key differences on how to use the *five challenging questions* when working with deep stories as opposed to the simpler stories we have worked with so far.

Remember that deep stories are much more ingrained than simpler stories and hence will feel more like facts/the Truth.

Question #1 – "How do you know that to (always) be true, *<your first name>?"*
There is emphasis on "always" when looking at deep stories:

- Think about your past. Can you find counterexamples to the story you are challenging? If so, the story cannot be True.
- If you are unable to find any counterexamples on your own, seek input from one or more people that you trust:
  o "I have this perception that <I am not a risk-taker (insert your deep story here)>, and I am curious if you have that same perception of me? Can you think of any examples where you perceive that <I took a risk (insert counterexample to your deep story here)>?"
- If you do not have anybody else to ask, or if they agree with your deep story, here is a fail-safe approach:
  o Ask yourself if you know this will "always" be true *in the future.* (You cannot know this. Neuroplasticity shows us that our brains are changing all the time!) At the very least this question should plant a shadow of a doubt in your mind about this deep story being a fact.

Question #2 – "What other valid stories could one create based upon the same observable data?"
- The "observable data" for deep stories is often less direct/tangible than with simpler stories; it can feel more conceptual and certainly cuts across time and situations.
- This will become clearer in the forthcoming examples.

Questions #3 and #4 – There are no differences in using either of these questions when working with deep (vs. non-deep) stories.

Question #5 – "How will you experiment with acting differently, *<your first name>?*

- For the simpler stories we have challenged so far, the action is often binary. You start doing something you are not doing or stop doing something you are doing. For deep stories, there are often multiple approaches you could experiment with, and you will typically ease your way into a change.

- There is a helpful technique I call the "three-step experimentation staircase."
  - Imagine a three-step staircase.
  - Label the first/bottom step as "low stakes" or "low risk." The second step is "medium stakes" or "medium risk" and the third/top step represents "high stakes" or "high risk."
  - As you brainstorm ideas for how to experiment with acting differently, you can metaphorically put each of those ideas on one of the three steps.
  - Always start experimenting at the bottom of the staircase by choosing lower-stakes opportunities.
  - Each of the three examples included in this chapter involve this three-step experimentation staircase.

As you experiment in low-stakes situations, you are creating new neural pathways that will allow you to more confidently **walk up the staircase** to higher-stakes situations—the ones with the biggest reward.

Challenging a Deep Story – A Personal Example

Let me share a personal example of how I worked through one of my own deep stories, "I am not a risk taker."

I have mentioned that deep stories really feel like the Truth. When somebody first suggested to me that my belief, "I am not a risk taker," was only a story, I was incensed. I pushed back, I was not open to this idea. "I know me. I know I am not a risk taker. How can this person have the gall to suggest I don't know myself?"

I share this because it can take time just to get to a place where you are even open to the possibility that a deep story is not a fact.

While it did take me some time to get there, once I was open to the possibility that "I am not a risk taker" might be a story, I was ready to use the *five challenging questions*.

The following represents the "conversation" I had with myself to challenge my story that "I am not a risk taker."

Question 1 – "How do you know that to (always) be true, *<Mike>?"*
- As I thought about whether this was always true for me in the past, I was able to identify some things (like having gone white water rafting many years ago or having recently quit

my job) that were actually a bit risky. This realization started to loosen my attachment to this being a fact.

Question 2 – "What other valid stories could one create based upon the same observable data?"

- In this situation, the "observable data" would be to consider situations where I had chosen not to take a risk.
- As I reflected on some of the more recent situations where I had avoided risk, I realized that two other possible stories (besides "I am not a risk taker") were that I might be (a) afraid of failure or (b) afraid of uncertainty. This further loosened my grip on the "fact" I was not a risk taker.
- Remember, we don't need to generate lots of other stories— just a few is enough to send the right signal to your brain.

Question 3 – "How might you act differently, <Mike>, if you didn't believe that story to be true?"

- I thought that if I no longer held on to the story that I was not a risk taker, I could take some risks. This may sound mundane, but it was *hugely* powerful for me!

Question 4 – "Do you think it would serve you to act that way, <Mike>?"

- A resounding YES.

Question 5 – "How will you experiment with acting differently, <Mike>?"

- I used the three-step experimentation staircase technique and mentally created a three-step staircase. I labeled the first step as "low-stakes," the middle step as "medium-stakes," and the top step as "high-stakes."
- I did not have any predefined scenarios or situations to slot into my staircase.
- I decided that as items came up that seemed risky, I would step back and determine which step on the staircase it belonged to. I created simple assessment criteria to use.
  - First, I considered how much I cared about the situation. If the presenting risk was in an arena that

was not important to me, there was no point in pursuing that risk any further. (This was an important insight for me. Just because I knew it would be valuable for me to be able to start taking more risks, this did not mean I should take any and all risks.)

- o Second, if the presenting risk pertained to something that was important to me, I considered what would be the worst thing that could happen if the risk back-fired. If the worst thing that could happen was not that bad, that translated into a "low-stakes" risk on my staircase; one worth taking as an experiment.

- A cool thing that happened for me as I started paying more attention to this is that I became hyper-aware of when I was about to say "no" to something because it seemed risky. This allowed me to pause, and then that inner coaching voice would kick in and say, "Hold on Mike, here is that story again. You know we are not so sure it is True. So, let's step back and assess this risk and see if it is one worth taking."

- As I began taking more low-stakes risks, it started building my own internal data/experience bank, giving me more and more evidence that I could be a risk-taker.
  - o On the neuroplasticity front, I was developing new neural pathways. My Ladder of Inference's Reflexive Loop, habitually saying no to anything risky, was weakening.
  - o Psychologically, I was becoming less and less beholden to my story that I was not a risk-taker.

- Over time I have become much more comfortable with risk. I no longer believe "I am not a risk taker." That self-imposed barrier is gone. I have created a new story I use to assess risks: "I will take risks if they are in service of my purpose."

- In some ways, it is funny for me to look back and think how strongly I believed that story to be a fact.

There is no way I would have launched Coach Your Self Up into the world if I had not challenged and busted through my story about not being a risk taker. This is a powerful example of how self-coaching can help tremendously on the career front. Shifting my behavior around risk-taking has clearly helped me tap into more of my potential.

Introducing the Self-Observation Worksheet

Now that you have learned about all of the steps involved in shifting a self-limiting behavior (SLB), here is a tool you can use to support your efforts. This Self-Observation Worksheet (see Image #1 on the following page) is designed to give you one place to consolidate your self-observation reflections pertaining to a selected SLB.

You can download an electronic copy of this worksheet on the Resources page of the coachyourselfup.com website.

The form includes a horizontal line that separates what we have been referring to as "outer" work (top section) and "inner" work (bottom section).

Seeing this delineation between the inner and outer work is a strong visual reminder of the importance of doing the inner work to support an outer (behavioral) change.

It also helps you to see that there are inner forces at play that support your current behavior. This gives you more insight into why making this particular change is not easy.

While the worksheet is generally self-explanatory, here are some suggestions on how to best utilize this tool.

- In the upper right section of the form, document the SLB you are intending to shift. The worksheet includes a brief reference to the selection criteria we discussed earlier.
- In the upper left section of the form, write down the "flipped" aspirational statement. This leverages the findings from the Intentional Change Theory that you are more likely to make and sustain a behavioral shift if it is in service of becoming the you that you aspire to be. The worksheet includes brief reminders of how to create a powerful aspirational statement.

IMAGE #1

COACH YOUR SELF UP®
SELF-OBSERVATION WORKSHEET

Aspirational Statement	Self-Limiting Behavior (SLB)
• A "flipped" version of your self-limiting behavior • You *believe* this helps you be a better you • Written in positive language, in the present tense	• A behavior you *want* to change • Change will yield a positive personal impact • Occurs relatively often (best for first learning to self-coach)

OUTER WORK
....
INNER WORK

Self-Observation Insights - What are you learning about yourself as you pay attention to your SLB?

Feelings & Triggers

Are there any strong feelings commonly associated with engaging in your SLB (e.g., anxiety, impatience, anger, etc...)?

Are you noticing any triggers (body, world or mind) that commonly precede your SLB?

Deep Stories

Assumptions or beliefs you have about yourself or your "world" that may underlie your SLB

Review the sample list of common deep stories in your program materials to see if any seem to connect to this SLB.

What concerns you about shifting this SLB? What might go wrong if you decreased or eliminated this SLB? (Your response may point to one or more stories.)

What benefit do you get from engaging in this SLB? (Your response may point to one or more stories.)

- Use the bottom half of the worksheet to capture key insights from your ongoing self-observation. The form includes multiple questions for you to consider as you seek to identify the feelings, triggers, and stories that underlie your identified SLB.
  - One question asks you to think about what concerns you about shifting this behavior or what might go wrong if you shifted this behavior. Asked another way, what benefit do you get from your SLB?
  - Answering those questions can help to reveal potential underlying stories that *support* you in continuing to engage in your SLB. We'll see how these questions come into play in the upcoming examples.
- As we discussed in prior chapters, having increased self-awareness about your SLB allows you to challenge any underlying stories (using the *five challenging questions*) and to begin to experiment with acting differently.

This worksheet is provided as a recommended aid. Capturing your thoughts in writing in some format, whether on this worksheet or in a journal or some other document you create, will positively impact your change efforts.

The way you prefer to utilize the tools and tactics shared in this book is entirely up to you. For illustrative purposes, I will use the Self-Observation Worksheet in the following examples.

Seeing this delineation between the inner and outer work is a strong visual reminder of the **importance of doing the inner work** to support an outer (behavioral) change.

> **Let's meet Bill, who cannot say "no", and Kelly, who does not speak up in meetings**
>
> Both of the following examples highlight (a) how an individual used the Self-Observation Worksheet to identify a deep story underlying their self-limiting behavior (SLB) and (b) how they then used the *five challenging questions* to challenge that deep story to pave the way for sustainable behavior change.

Example #1 - Bill cannot say "no" to taking on more work – what lies underneath?

This is from a person who had an SLB of always saying "yes" to new tasks and projects at work. We will call this person Bill.

Let's look at Bill's Self-Observation Worksheet in chunks.

On the top of the form (Image #2), you can see how Bill articulated his SLB and his "flipped" aspirational statement.

- SLB – I'm unable to say "no" (when it's a viable and reasonable option).
- "Flipped" aspirational statement – I am comfortable saying "no" when it serves me to do so.

The bottom of the form captures some of the key insights Bill had during a multi-week self-observation period.

Feelings & Triggers: (Image #3) With a bit of tongue-in-cheek flavor, Bill highlighted that the key trigger here is receiving a request from another person. Beyond that (obvious) note, he noticed that he feels varying levels of anxiety once the request has been made. He equated increasing levels of anxiety with increasing levels of desire to say no.

IMAGE #2

COACH YOUR SELF UP®
SELF-OBSERVATION WORKSHEET

Aspirational Statement	Self-Limiting Behavior (SLB)
I am comfortable saying "no" when it serves me to do so	I'm unable to say "no" (when it's a viable and reasonable option)
• A "flipped" version of your self-limiting behavior • You *believe* this helps you be a better you • Written in positive language, in the present tense	• A behavior you *want* to change • Change will yield a positive personal impact • Occurs relatively often (best for first learning to self-coach)

OUTER WORK

IMAGE #3

INNER WORK

Self-Observation Insights
What are you learning about yourself as you pay attention to your SLB?

Feelings & Triggers

Are there any strong feelings commonly associated with engaging in your SLB (e.g., anxiety, impatience, anger, etc...)?

Are you noticing any triggers (body, world or mind) that commonly precede your SLB?

• *Funny, the obvious trigger here is somebody else asking me to do something. That said, I do notice that I feel varying levels of anxiety rise up as I'm in the conversation. As I've been self-observing, I see that the more anxious I feel, the more I wish I could say no.*

151

Deep Stories: (Image #4) While he captured several different insights in this section, they all pointed to Bill's awareness that he believed he needed to be liked by everybody he worked with AND if he were to say "no" to anybody they would no longer like him.

IMAGE #4

INNER WORK

Self-Observation Insights

**What are you learning about yourself as
you pay attention to your SLB?**

Deep Stories

**Assumptions or beliefs you have about yourself or your "world"
that may underlie your SLB**

Review the sample list of common deep stories in your program materials to see if any seem to connect to this SLB.

What concerns you about shifting this SLB? What might go wrong if you decreased or eliminated this SLB? (Your response may point to one or more stories.)

What benefit do you get from engaging in this SLB? (Your response may point to one or more stories.)

- From the sample list, "I need to be liked by everybody I work with" feels like it could be related.

- Concerns - I worry that if I say no, the person who asked me for help will see me as <u>not</u> being a team player. They will think less of me and potentially not like me (as much or at all).

- Benefits - People like me, they know they can count on me.

- I'm spread super thin and working crazy hours. So while there is a nice benefit here, there's also a lot of pain. I need to say "no" sometimes, to better manage my boundaries. I think the fact is I'm uncomfortable with being disliked and I keep saying "yes" so as not to rock the boat with anyone. I guess I need to challenge this (although I think it will be hard and this just feels like how I am wired).

I have mentioned that there are often multiple layers to our stories. This is an interesting example of at least two layered stories. On one level, Bill had a story that saying "no" would lead to people disliking him. On another deeper level, he had a story that he needed to be liked by everyone.

I advocate challenging the deeper story, as that often will provide more transformational benefits. Trust your instincts that you can identify the deeper story if you find layered stories.

You can see from Bill's notes on his worksheet that while he saw that he needed to challenge this deeper belief that he needed to be liked by everyone, he was pretty sure this is just how he is wired—so he did not think this was a story.

Reminder - the purpose of the Self-Observation Worksheet is to identify if there are one or more stories that underlie your selected SLB. If one or more stories are revealed, you then use the five challenging questions to challenge those stories and begin to experiment with acting differently.

Let's now shift gears and follow along with Bill as he challenged his deep story that, "I need everybody to like me."

This dialogue represents Bill's self-talk.

Question 1 – "How do you know that to (always) be true, *<Bill>*?"

- This felt a bit tricky for Bill to answer. In thinking about the correlation between his inability to say "no" and *"needing everybody to like him,"* Bill decided to focus on his tendency to put the needs of others before his own, which included his tendency to say "yes." Could he think of situations where he ever put himself first (e.g., by saying "no")?

- He remembered that last year he had a difficult personal situation to deal with and had to be firm in managing his own boundaries to allow himself time to focus on the situation. This reminded him that there had been a few personal situations in the last five years that he treated similarly. During those instances, he had to say "no" to some things and upon reflection was concerned at the time that some people might not like him for it, but he had said "no" anyway.

- This startled Bill a bit, since he had this sense that he <u>never</u> said "no." This led him to reflect on the notion that while he definitely *wanted* the people he worked with to like him, maybe he did not *need* them to.

Question 2 – "What other valid stories could one create based upon the same observable data?"

- In Bill's case, he reflected on the situations when he had said "yes" to things where in hindsight he wished he had said "no." Might there be other explanations other than needing (or even wanting) to be liked?
- He determined that it was possible in some cases that he said "yes" because he thought saying "no" could have been seen as a sign of weakness, a sign that he was not up to the challenge.
- He thought it was possible he had been trying to protect his reputation as a person who could always be counted on.

Bill still felt strongly he preferred to have other people like him, but he started to feel more open to the notion that his original premise, his belief that he was wired to need people to like him, was maybe not a "fact."

Question 3 – "How might you act differently, *<Bill>*, if you didn't believe that story to be true?"

- Bill noted he would do a better job of managing his boundaries to take care of himself and his own needs.
- Bill knew he was *not* interested in saying "no" all the time. He knew he did *not* intend to act in a way that suggested he did not care about people's feelings or how others felt about him. Bill would continue to be sensitive to the needs of others and help out when he could. And he would better prioritize his own needs.

Question 4 – "Do you think it would serve you to act that way, *<Bill>*?"

- Yes. While still a bit scary as this seemed like such a big shift, Bill recognized it could be hugely positive for him if he could start moving the needle on this behavior.

Question 5 – "How will you experiment with acting differently, *<Bill>*?"

- Bill did some research on "boundary management" by searching for articles and blogs and found some helpful resources. He found some great ideas on how to say "no" in a respectful and supportive manner, which made him more comfortable when thinking about his experiments.

- Although it felt a bit risky, Bill thought it was important for his manager (Sue) to be aware of this shift that he wanted to make. He would share his ideas with her and see if she had any insights to share with him based on her experience and her knowledge of both Bill and the organization.

- Bill liked the idea of using the "staircase" technique and having a three-step staircase ("low-stakes," "medium-stakes," and "high-stakes") for assessing situations for possible experimentation with saying "no."

- Bill identified some simple criteria he would use to assess inquiries as they came to him.
  - *Criterion 1 – Who was making the request?* There were a handful of things to consider here. How important was Bill's working relationship with the requestor? What was the "political" (organizational politics) stature of the requestor? And so on. Less important working relationships and individuals with less internal clout would be associated with "low stakes" situations that were ripe for initial experimentation with saying "no."
  - *Criterion 2 – What was the size of the request, i.e., how much effort was involved?* Less effort would be "lower stakes" as the requestor would be less negatively impacted if Bill were to say "no."

- o *Criterion 3 – What other options existed?* More additional options, e.g., there were other individuals with the capability to take on the work, equated to "lower stakes."
- Bill became much more aware of and thoughtful about requests for his time and effort. Another tactic he started to employ early on was to let the requestor know that he needed a bit of time to process the request. This gave him time to reflect on his criteria and to think about his "messaging" in cases where he declined to help out.
- Reactions from requestors were all over the map when Bill would say "no." (And Bill was providing more context than just declining to help.)
  - o Some requestors were fine with it.
  - o Others got upset and moved on. Bill had a tough time dealing with the fact that these people were upset, but he continued to work on being less attached to his story of needing everyone to like him.
  - o Some situations were escalated to his boss when the requestor found Bill's "no" response unacceptable. There was some tension here—and yet all of the situations were resolved.

While Bill feels like he will always be working on this, he believes he is **much better at managing his boundaries now** than he was when he started with his experiments a few months ago.

Example #2 - Kelly does not speak up in meetings – what lies underneath?

Let's walk through another example. This is from a person who had a self-limiting behavior (SLB) of not speaking up in meetings, even when she felt like she had something to contribute. For our purposes, we will call this person Kelly.

Let's look at Kelly's Self-Observation Worksheet in chunks.

On the top of the form (Image #5), you can see how Kelly articulated her SLB and her (flipped) aspirational statement.

- SLB – I don't speak up in meetings, even when there's something I want to say.
- "Flipped" aspirational statement – I am comfortable sharing my POV (point-of-view) in meetings.

IMAGE #5

COACH YOUR SELF UP®
SELF-OBSERVATION WORKSHEET

Aspirational Statement	Self-Limiting Behavior (SLB)
I am comfortable sharing my POV in meetings	I don't speak up in meetings, even when there's something I want to say
• A "flipped" version of your self-limiting behavior • You *believe* this helps you be a better you • Written in positive language, in the present tense	• A behavior you *want* to change • Change will yield a positive personal impact • Occurs relatively often (best for first learning to self-coach)

OUTER WORK
....

The bottom of the form captures some of the key insights Kelly had during a multi-week self-observation period.

Feelings & Triggers: (Image #6) Kelly identified that her initial trigger is the "thought of being nervous" which for her precedes physical sensations associated with her nervousness. Kelly noted she knows when she is not speaking up.

IMAGE #6

INNER WORK

Self-Observation Insights

What are you learning about yourself as you pay attention to your SLB?

Feelings & Triggers

Are there any strong feelings commonly associated with engaging in your SLB (e.g., anxiety, impatience, anger, etc...)?

Are you noticing any triggers (body, world or mind) that commonly precede your SLB?

- *I notice that my heart starts to beat faster when I've got something I want to say in a meeting. I feel nervous. There's also a feeling like butterflies in my stomach.*
- *The thought of being nervous because I have something I'd like to say definitely precedes the faster heart beat and the butterflies. The idea of speaking up leads to the physical signs of nervousness.*
- *It's safe to say I am aware of when I have something I'd like to share.*

Deep Stories: (Image #7) Kelly came to realize she had a fear that her ideas would be rejected and that would lead others to reject her as well. This was based on personal experience as she could think of a few situations, including some back in high school, where she had spoken up and had felt personally rejected in the process. Kelly found it better to play it safe by not speaking up.

IMAGE #7

INNER WORK

Self-Observation Insights

What are you learning about yourself as you pay attention to your SLB?

Deep Stories

Assumptions or beliefs you have about yourself or your "world" that may underlie your SLB

Review the sample list of common deep stories in your program materials to see if any seem to connect to this SLB.

What concerns you about shifting this SLB? What might go wrong if you decreased or eliminated this SLB? (Your response may point to one or more stories.)

What benefit do you get from engaging in this SLB? (Your response may point to one or more stories.)

- *In reviewing the sample list of deep stories, the idea that I will be judged harshly resonates with me. I'm concerned that if others don't like my ideas, they may no longer view me as a credible team member.*

- *The benefit I get from not speaking up is that I do not open myself up for potential rejection.*

- *I can see I have a story here that others will no longer see me as a credible team member if they don't like my ideas. I need to challenge this story if I ever hope to be comfortable sharing my ideas in meetings.*

She realized that while she knew this was self-limiting, her tendency to not speak up protected her from the potential negative experience of being rejected. She saw that this deep story was at the root of her SLB and knew for her to shift her SLB, she would need to challenge that story.

Kelly decided that even though she felt this story was True (that she would be rejected by others along with her ideas), she was willing to use the *five challenging questions* to challenge it.

Let's now shift gears and follow along with Kelly as she challenged her deep story that, "I will be rejected by others along with my ideas."

This dialogue represents Kelly's self-talk.

Question 1 – "How do you know that to (always) be true, *<Kelly>*?"

- As Kelly reflected on her past, she could think of a few meetings here and there where she had spoken up and her ideas were welcomed. But still, those were quite a while ago and involved cases where she felt more confident about the subject matter and her standing with her colleagues.

- So even though she could accept that this story was not *always* true, it still felt true in her current work setting.

- Kelly decided to ask her most trusted colleague for his opinion on the matter. He noted she was so quiet in meetings he had a hard time thinking of counterexamples. However, he strongly disagreed with her story about what she thought would happen. "Sure Kelly, your idea may not win the day. For me that feels really different than your idea being rejected. That seems like a harsh way to view that. And I don't believe folks around here will reject you as a person just because they may not agree with your input." He also noted he thought it would help Kelly, not hinder her, to participate more in meetings. He knew some folks wondered about her level of engagement due to her lack of speaking up in group discussions.

- This was an interesting perspective from her colleague. Kelly was intrigued to consider that her perceptions of how others would react might be limiting her contributions. And her current practice of not speaking up might be leading others to think less of her—exactly what she was trying to avoid.

Question 2 – "What other valid stories could one create based upon the same observable data?"

- In Kelly's case, she did not feel she needed to work through this question.
- Since Kelly saw the value in challenging her current situation, she was *open-minded* to the possibility that her belief (that others would reject her along with her ideas) was a story.

Question 3 – "How might you act differently, <*Kelly*>, if you didn't believe that story to be true?"

- Kelly noted she would start speaking up more in meetings. Especially when she had something that felt relevant to the discussion topic at hand.

Question 4 – "Do you think it would serve you to act that way, <*Kelly*>?"

- Kelly thought this would definitely be good for her. She would love to be more comfortable sharing her ideas.

Question 5 – "How will you experiment with acting differently, <*Kelly*>?"

- Using the "staircase" technique, Kelly created a three-step staircase ("low-stakes," "medium-stakes," and "high-stakes").
- Kelly identified several recurring scenarios to put on her staircase. Here is what she came up with as a first cut:
  - Low-stakes conversations/meetings:
    - One-on-one conversations with Sue, Raman, Devon, and Angie;
    - Weekly team status meetings;
    - Meetings with the Quality Assurance team.
  - Medium-stakes conversations/meetings:

- One-on-one conversations with Jennifer (boss), Jeff, Alex, Trudy, and Tyler;
  - Periodic meetings – Project ABC;
  - Meetings with the Hardware team.
- High-stakes conversations/meetings:
  - Product design meetings;
  - Product marketing meetings;
  - Any meetings that involved a senior leader.

- This gave Kelly a roadmap for which meetings she would use to experiment with speaking up. As she started to speak up in the low-stakes meetings, she paid particular attention to whether or not her belief that "I will be rejected along with my ideas" was True (capital T).

- As it turned out, most of the time Kelly's ideas were simply pulled into the general conversation. There were certainly times that others challenged or identified flaws in her ideas, but she did not perceive she was being personally rejected.

- Over the course of six months or so, Kelly "climbed the experimentation staircase" and is now much more participative in meetings across the board.

This gave Kelly **a roadmap for which meetings she would use to experiment with speaking up**. As she started to speak up in the low-stakes meetings, she paid particular attention to whether or not her belief that "I will be rejected along with my ideas" was True (capital T).

Experiments Require Intention, Attention, and Reflection

I want to explicitly state a point that has been implied throughout. When you experiment with acting differently, it is critical that you are consciously engaged.

First, you are conducting an intentional act. You are intentionally trying on a new behavior, a new way of responding.

Second, you are paying attention to yourself and to your environment while you are in the experiment. Trust yourself to pay attention to the most important things in the moment. Using Kelly's example, if she speaks up and others engage her in dialogue, her primary focus will be on participating in the dialogue. If she focuses too much on having a conversation with herself about "Hey, this is cool, they are not rejecting my ideas…" she will not be as present as she could be to the conversation.

Hence the importance of the third leg of this stool—reflection. At some point after the experiment (the sooner the better), it is helpful to reflect upon your experience. What went well? What did not go well? What insights can you apply to your next experiment? Does this change your sense of what you consider low /medium/high stakes scenarios? And so on.

As usual, I advocate that you capture these reflections in writing.

Short-Cutting the *Five Challenging Questions*

When a child learns to ride a bike, she uses training wheels. After a period of time, as she becomes more adept with the skills needed to balance the bike on her own, it is time to take the training wheels off. They were critical to her success at learning to ride but became unnecessary and even inefficient as she gained more skill. At some point, it is easier to ride without the training wheels on.

Questions #1 and #2 are like training wheels. As you become more adept at seeing stories (simple or deep) in your life, questions #1 and #2 become less important and even unnecessary.

Here are the *five challenging questions* again for easy reference.

> Five challenging questions:
>
> 1. How do you know that to (always) be true, *<your first name>*?
>
> 2. What other valid stories could one create based upon the same observable data?
>
> 3. How might you act differently, *<your first name>*, if you didn't believe that story to be true?
>
> 4. Do you think it would serve you to act that way, *<your first name>*?
>
> 5. How will you experiment with acting differently, *<your first name>*?

Questions #1 and #2 are like **training wheels**. As you become more adept at seeing stories (simple or deep) in your life, **questions #1 and #2 become less important and even unnecessary**.

The purpose of questions #1 and #2 is to help you become open to the possibility that something you believe to be the Truth (capital T) is in fact only a story.

As soon as you successfully challenge and start to shift one of your deep stories, you will become more open-minded to the possibility that other beliefs you have about yourself might also be stories ripe to be challenged.

For example, you may notice that <your need to be liked by everybody you work with> (simply an illustrative example) underlies your self-limiting behavior of "not being able to say no." Instead of spending the time and energy contemplating and answering questions #1 and #2, you will just think, "Although it feels like a fact to me, maybe this idea that I need everyone to like me is a deep story. How might I act differently if I did not believe that story to be true, <your first name>?" Boom, you have just taken a short-cut right to question #3.

Your Own Work

Each attempt to challenge a deep story will be a unique situation. I shared the three examples in this chapter to give you a sense of different ways the experience might unfold.

You understand the steps to follow as you use the self-coaching path to sustainable behavior change:

- Strengthen your ability to manage your attention.
- Use your attention to watch yourself, to self-observe the self-limiting behavior (SLB) you want to shift. Periodically reflect upon and write down your self-observations. Use the Self-Observation Worksheet if that form works for you.
- Once you identify one or more underlying stories, challenge them and begin to experiment with acting differently.

Remember to meet yourself where you are and to practice self-compassion. Beating yourself up is unhelpful. Change takes time. Be patient. And sustainable change requires that you do the inner work to support the outer change. Trust the process.

As soon as you successfully challenge and start to shift one of your deep stories, you will become more open-minded to the possibility that **other beliefs you have about yourself might also be stories** ripe to be challenged.

CHAPTER 11 SUMMARY

Challenging Deep Stories - Examples and Tactics

- There are differences on how to use the *five challenging questions* when working with deep stories as opposed to non-deep stories.

- The "three-step experimentation staircase" is a helpful technique to identify opportunities for experimenting with acting differently.

- Always start out at the bottom of the staircase with low-stakes situations. This will build confidence to climb the staircase to higher stakes (and higher reward) scenarios.

- The Self-Observation Worksheet is an optional tool we can use to support our behavior change efforts.

- The Self-Observation Worksheet provides a visual reminder of the importance of doing the inner work that is necessary to support the outer behavioral change.

- With more practice and awareness, we will be more open to the possibility that our beliefs are stories. Questions #1 and #2 of the *five challenging questions* become unnecessary.

"Being Here" Activity

Managing Attention – Focus on Your Body

Sit up in your chair with both feet on the ground. You should be comfortable, but not slouched over. Take a few deep breaths.

With your eyes closed, focus your attention on your hands. (If you have a disability that makes this activity impossible for you, improvise by focusing on some other bodily sensation.)

Wiggle your fingers one at a time. Notice each finger as you wiggle it. Wiggle all of your fingers together.

On both hands, touch your thumbs to your index fingers. Hold for a few seconds and focus your attention on how it feels where they are touching.

Repeat with touching your thumbs to your middle fingers. Then thumbs to fourth fingers. And finally, with thumbs to your pinkie fingers.

Now wiggle all your fingers again before relaxing both hands.

While doing this, when you become distracted by a thought, a sound, or another bodily sensation, just acknowledge it, and gently let it go. Bring your attention back to your hands.

This should take 30-60 seconds.

When you are ready, take one last deep breath and gently open your eyes and come back into your space.

Chapter 12

Getting Unstuck

Before you read on, I invite you to take a minute and get a bit more *present* by engaging in the "Being Here" activity on the prior page. You will practice using your superpower of managing attention to focus on your body. This will help to get you "here" mentally.

Using Self-Coaching to Get Unstuck

I had been happily cranking along with my efforts to write this book. After all, I have been teaching this program for a few years and I was simply translating that into book form.

However, I knew that one of the benefits of writing this book was that I would be able to add additional material that went beyond the classroom program. As I got to the point where I was shifting into the new content, I started losing momentum and motivation.

My coach encouraged me to apply my self-coaching tools to this situation. I told her that my self-coaching approach was intended to help people shift their self-limiting behaviors, not to help move through periods of being stuck.

She challenged me to reconsider this. In that moment, I realized I had made up a story about how or where these self-coaching skills apply. Sure, I had designed the program with a specific intent—and that was a fact. However, I could be open to the possibility there was something more here.

I went to the *five challenging questions* to challenge my story that "self-coaching skills are not geared toward getting unstuck." Being adept with the process, I was able to skip the first two questions (See Short-Cutting the *Five Challenging Questions* on page 163) since I was already comfortable that this was a story. It was then a simple process from there to have this conversation with myself:

Question #3 - "How might you act differently, *Mike,* if you didn't believe this story to be true?"
- "If I did not believe that self-coaching skills were *not* helpful in getting unstuck, I would try to apply them to my current situation" (feeling stuck and not moving forward on my book).

Question #4 – "Do you think it would serve you to act in that way, *Mike?*"
- "YES! I want to move forward!"

Question #5 – "How will you experiment with acting differently, *Mike?*"
- "I'll just do it. I will try to apply self-coaching skills to my current situation and see if that helps."

I pulled out the Self-Observation Worksheet. Here is some of the information I captured there:

Self-Limiting Behavior – "Not finishing the book / feel stuck."

Aspirational Statement – "I am motivated and doing whatever it takes to publish this book."

Feelings & Triggers – "Anytime I think about writing, my energy feels depleted; I feel a sense of malaise."

Deep Stories –
- "Benefit of <u>not</u> shifting my SLB – (1) my work is shielded from public scrutiny and potential criticism; (2) I do not have to create the new content (which I think will be hard to write)."

I realized I had **made up a story** about how or where these self-coaching skills apply. I could be open to the possibility **there was something more here**.

As I reflected on this, I realized that I was having some doubts about whether this content was really book-worthy or maybe more importantly, was I author-worthy?

Ok. This revealed a number of potential stories that might be blocking me from moving forward:

1. "This content is not book-worthy." Wow, I respect that I am having those thoughts, but I would not have started writing this book if I did not think this content was powerful and would be helpful to many people. Anytime I start questioning the value of my content, I simply need to remind myself of how much this has helped people in the classroom. This potential story is not blocking me.

2. "I am not author-worthy." Ok, I may not be a born writer, but I have worthy material to share. In fact, I believe this is one of the gifts I have been tasked with bringing to the world. And what makes somebody author-worthy anyway? I do not think this potential story is blocking me.

3. "I am afraid of public scrutiny." I am naturally predisposed to please others—I want others to like me. This one caused some deeper reflection. Could it be that deep down I am afraid that if I publish this book I run the risk of having people judge me harshly? While it intellectually makes sense this would be at play, it just does not feel like this potential story is blocking me.

4. "I don't know how to create the final pieces of content to get me to the finish line. It's too hard." Bang! As I pondered this one, I heard a voice inside me say, "Yes, that's it. It was easy to write about your program, but adding extra stuff is hard. And not only will it be hard, but it will be hard to ensure it is good. And we *(that would be me, myself and I)* do not want to have our name on something that is not good."

Ok, so in this instance, the fourth time was the charm. I believe I found the key story that was keeping me stuck.

Now to challenge this story! I skipped the first two challenging questions as I have been working this type of material long enough to immediately jump to the conclusion that "I am working with a story here." Here's the brief conversation I had with myself:

> Question #3 - "How might you act differently, *Mike*, if you didn't believe this story to be true?"
> - "If I did not believe that it would be too hard to create the final pieces of content for my book, I would jump back into writing."
>
> Question #4 – "Do you think it would serve you to act in that way, *Mike*?"
> - "YES!"
>
> Question #5 – "How will you experiment with acting differently, *Mike*?"
> - "It's time to jump back in. I am going to commit to spending at least 10 hours per week on writing."

That was a key turning point for me.

Summary Tips for Using Self-Coaching to Get Unstuck

Ironically, as you read in the previous pages, I used self-coaching to (a) shift my belief that self-coaching would not be helpful in getting unstuck and then (b) used self-coaching to get unstuck.

Here is a quick summary of how you can try this in your own life:
1. Become aware that you are stuck.
2. Use your self-observation/self-reflection skills to identify one or more stories that might be blocking you. Use your judgment as to whether or not to use the Self-Observation Worksheet or some sort of journaling. Remember that writing things down has a positive impact on the process.
3. Use the *five challenging questions* to challenge the story/stories and identify how you will experiment with acting differently.
4. Experiment with acting differently.

CHAPTER 12 SUMMARY

Getting Unstuck

- Self-coaching can help us get unstuck.

- As we get better at noticing stories, we can assess whether there are any stories that are causing us to feel stuck.

- If we can identify a story that underlies our feeling stuck, we can use the *five challenging questions* to identify one or more actions to experiment with acting differently.

Chapter 13

Maintaining Momentum and Moving Forward

We have covered a lot of ground in our time together.

One challenge with training programs is that once the formal course is over, we tend to go back to the way things were and fall back into our old patterns.

Coach Your Self Up is designed to be "sticky," to help the material stick with you.

- The key learning points were shared in bite-sized chunks.
- You were encouraged to step away from the book multiple times to engage in Learning Practices. This reinforced the key learning points and started to develop your self-coaching skills.
- If you had the luxury of working through this book with one or more accountability partners, that was an added boost.

I find it is important for individuals to brainstorm ways that they can hold the gains that they have made <u>and</u> continue to maintain momentum on making forward progress on their own.

Following is a list of the types of ideas that have come up most frequently. Scan through these items and decide which will work best for you. Or maybe this list will trigger some new ideas that feel even better for you and your circumstances.

Scan through these items and decide which will work best **for you**.

- **Block time on your calendar to work on specific tasks (single-tasking).** This is an underutilized tactic for getting focused work done. We are great at putting appointments on our calendars when they involve other people. Why not make appointments with ourselves for important tasks?
    - o Flavor 1 – Schedule time to focus on your work priorities (e.g., block an hour to work on Project ABC).
    - o Flavor 2 – Schedule time to focus on your personal development (e.g., schedule 15-30-minutes per week for reflection and/or journaling).
- **Set your smartphone on airplane mode** during times when you want to focus.
- **Set your email to NOT alert you when you get a new email.** Many people find it next to impossible to resist looking at a newly received email. This can be a huge distraction or interruption. Consider doing this at all times, and at the very least during times of focus.
- Create a **visual signal** that others can see that conveys, "No interruptions please."
    - o At one of my prior employers, we all had New Year's Eve style party hats. We agreed on a way to position those hats in/on our cubicles such that they conveyed to others whether we were "open" for visitors or not.
- Implement **meeting kick-off practices** for your team or department.

- ○ Some groups start each meeting with some time (typically one to a few minutes) spent sitting in silence—with the intention of becoming more present for the meeting.
- ○ Some groups start each meeting by going around the room and asking people to briefly "check in." These practices force people to become more present to their current state.
  - One variation is to have people use one word to describe their current emotional state.
  - Another variation is to have people briefly acknowledge what else is pulling on their attention that is getting in their way of being present. This practice can also help to develop empathy as group members gain insight into the challenges others are facing.
- Work with **an accountability partner or group**. If you know any others who have read this book, or you think would be interested in this kind of personal development work, ask if they would like to engage with you to provide each other mutual support and accountability on your improvement efforts. (If you worked through this book with others, consider whether you want to continue working together.)
- **Seek feedback**—from people that you trust—to help shine a light on your blind spot. Use this approach to identify self-limiting behaviors (SLBs) that you are not aware of. Consider sharing the sample list of SLBs from this book (see page 62) with the individual(s) from whom you are seeking feedback. This may make it easier for them to identify an opportunity for you to improve.
- **Always be working on one self-limiting behavior (SLB)**. Focus on that SLB for 3-6 months until you are comfortable with the shifts you have made.
- Create some sort of **visual reminder** that you can put near your computer or on your desk or refrigerator (i.e., somewhere you will see it often) to help keep this work top-of-mind.

- **Be on the lookout for stories**. Notice where you are making assumptions that you treat like facts.
  - One technique that I use almost daily and highly recommend is to **use the phrase, "This is the story I told myself."** For example, I might say to a colleague, "We didn't make the deadline, and *this is the story I told myself* about why that happened." Then I go on to share the story I have told myself.
    - This technique is powerful as it conveys to others—even those who have had no exposure to the concept of stories—that I can see where I am making things up. This ensures that others understand *my* perception and invites them to share *theirs*.
    - As I put this technique into practice, it led me to see that I make up stories about so many things every day.
  - Another idea is to spend a few minutes each week **reflecting on a current situation where you feel stuck** and thinking about what stories you have that could be impacting the situation.
- **Revisit this book periodically** and review items of interest.
- **Search out other relevant resources** pertaining to those aspects of personal growth that you find most interesting. This could include books, articles, movies, videos, etc. There is a list of recommended resources at the end of this book that includes a number of items to consider.
- Start a **book club**. Find others that are interested in reading books on one or more aspects of this type of content. The list of recommended resources at the end of this book includes a number of books to consider.
- **Attend a personal growth conference or weekend retreat.**
- Experiment with **meditation** (see the Other Helpful Personal Development Practices section just a few pages ahead).
- Experiment with ongoing **journaling** (ditto).
- Experiment with a **gratitude** practice (ditto).

One technique that I use almost daily and highly recommend is to **use the phrase, "This is the story I told myself."**

This technique is powerful as it conveys to others— even those who have had no exposure to the concept of stories—**that I can see where I am making things up.**

This ensures that others **understand *my* perception** and **invites them to share *theirs*.**

The Power of Mental Rehearsal (aka Visualization)

Another idea for maintaining momentum with this work is that of mental rehearsal. This is the practice of preparing in your own mind for a given event/situation and envisioning it happening in a positive way.

This is a common approach for professional athletes in all sports.

A somewhat famous example of this involves Laura Wilkinson, a US Olympic diver.

Six months prior to the 2000 Summer Olympics, Wilkinson suffered a serious foot injury that kept her out of action for a couple of months. During this time, she used mental images to visualize her dives. She pictured each step of each dive in her head.

Her foot was not fully recovered by the time she started diving again, but she was able to qualify for the Olympics. At the 2000 Summer Olympics, she earned the first gold medal for a female American platform diver since 1964.

Not only is performance positively impacted by mental rehearsal, brain studies have shown that imagining an activity in vivid detail *fires the same brain circuitry that is involved when the activity is being physically performed.*

How does this apply to you? You can use mental rehearsal to imagine being in a situation where you are likely to engage in your SLB and imagine acting/responding differently.

For example, you are working on interrupting others less often and you know you have an important one-on-one meeting coming up with somebody that you are prone to interrupt. You could imagine that meeting taking place, and imagine the person saying something he is likely to say that typically triggers you to interrupt. You can imagine yourself choosing to listen instead.

When you are in that meeting and the person says that thing that typically triggers you, your mental rehearsal will increase the odds that you will not interrupt. For the brain, it is like, "We have done this before."

You can use mental rehearsal to imagine being in a situation where you are likely to engage in your SLB and **imagine acting/responding differently.**

Other Helpful Personal Development Practices

Here are some other techniques to consider (a) integrating into your life on an ongoing basis and/or (b) utilizing to help you move forward in challenging times.

Meditation

There is a significant amount of research that highlights the benefits of meditation. (Check out the entry "Research on Meditation" on Wikipedia for a nice overview: en.wikipedia.org/wiki/research_on_meditation.) Meditation has been shown to have a positive effect on both physical and emotional well-being.

In the context of our self-coaching approach, the most direct connection is to *managing attention*. While there are many different approaches to meditation, they all include an emphasis on managing your attention—to have some object of desired attention (breath, bodily sensation, visualizations) and to notice when your attention has drifted away from the desired object and gently bring it back.

Meditation is one way to continue to cultivate your superpower of Managing Attention.

Meditation is also very effective for "grounding" or "centering" yourself and returning to a sense of peace and calm, even against a backdrop of hyperactivity and chaos.

I have included multiple references to resources on this topic in the Resources section at the back of this book.

While there are many different approaches to meditation, they all include an emphasis on **managing your attention**.

Journaling

As I hope you experienced with many aspects of Coach Your Self Up, there is power in writing things down.

Journaling practices vary from being focused on a specific topic all the way to capturing anything and everything about your current life experience.

You might be surprised at what flows out of your pen (or keyboard) when you give yourself permission to "dump" whatever is coming up for you.

Often times you will find ideas emerging that you had not thought of before.

Journaling can help to clear your mind and give you more space to step back and reassess a situation.

Expressing Gratitude

If you are reading this book, I am confident that you have things to be grateful for. We can start with the fact that you know how to read and are able to use that skill for personal benefit.

Numerous research studies have demonstrated the power of gratitude. (Check out this article from the Greater Good Science Center at UC Berkeley that provides links to relevant research findings:
greatergood.berkeley.edu/topic/gratitude/definition#why-practice). Expressing gratitude has been shown to improve mental, physical, and relational well-being.

Expressing gratitude can be especially helpful when you are feeling sad or frustrated. It is a great way to help put things in perspective.

The practice can be as simple as identifying three, five, ten (pick a number) things you are grateful for. Family, friends, health, shelter, running water, trees, birds, and so on. You can write them down or simply say them aloud.

Go ahead and try this right now. **Say out loud five things you are grateful for.** Take your time, do not rush it. Take a few seconds after each statement to let it soak in.

Did you notice you felt better afterwards? I cannot think of a time I have engaged in this practice where I did not feel better afterwards. My girlfriend and I often do this practice together by going back and forth and sharing things we are each grateful for.

A twist that I encourage you to add in periodically is to identify *qualities about yourself* that you are grateful for. Most of us do not spend much time acknowledging ourselves in this way. This is a powerful way to remind yourself how awesome you are!

Reminder – Target Outcomes

I invite you to flip back to pages 7-9 in this book and briefly review the target outcomes we identified at the beginning of this journey.

If you followed along and completed the suggested Learning Practices, it is likely that you have made shifts on all of those target outcomes. It is also likely that one or two of those outcomes feels especially prominent for you.

Journaling

Final Reflection – Personal Takeaways / Action Planning

I invite you to take a few minutes to reflect on the following questions and write down your thoughts in your journal.

- What has been most useful for me from my experience with Coach Your Self Up?
- What one or two things will I *commit to* doing for myself to hold on to any gains and keep moving forward?

Wrapping-Up?

When working with a group, I show them the following image—a hallway of open doors—as we are wrapping up.

On the one hand, there is a sense of closure in that the formal course has ended. On the other hand, for many, this is just the beginning of a potentially lifelong journey of raising their self-awareness and continuing on their path of self-discovery and continued professional and personal development.

I defer to your wisdom and intuition to determine what **future steps** you will take on your path.

A Few Final Things

I publish an *email newsletter* that comes out periodically, no more than once a month. It typically includes a handful of relevant blogs, articles or quotes from other sources, as well as my own blog posts. If you are interested in receiving my newsletter, you can sign up for that on the coachyouselfup.com website.

I invite you to peruse the Appendices and Resources ahead:

Appendix A – Hear from People Who Have Coached Themselves Up
- Includes personal stories from individuals who have benefited from the Coach Your Self Up training program.

Appendix B – Organizational Application
- Includes thoughts about the role that self-coaching and Coach Your Self Up can play inside of organizations.

Resources
- Includes a list of recommended books, websites, and a few TED talk videos.

Thank You and Good Luck

I am grateful you put in the time and effort to work through this book. I hope that you have added several self-coaching tools to your professional and personal development toolkit, and I wish you good luck in applying these skills to help you maximize your success.

Ever forward.

Invitation to Endorse *Coach Your Self Up*

If you found this book to be valuable, please consider taking a few minutes to provide a rating on Amazon. As a self-published author with dreams of making a big impact in the world, every positive endorsement makes a difference.

Check Out the eLearning version of Coach Your Self Up

coachyourselfup.com/course/paperback

CHAPTER 13 SUMMARY

Maintaining Momentum and Moving Forward

- It's important to commit to some ongoing practices to hold the gains we have made and keep moving forward with this work.

- There are many optional practices to consider—this chapter identifies more than a dozen.

- Write down one or two practices that you commit to.

Appendix A

Hear from People Who Have Coached Themselves Up

The following stories are from individuals who have participated in the Coach Your Self Up classroom program. I thought it could be inspiring for you to get a sense of the different ways this program is having a positive impact on people.

Alex Harris, President

All of the Coach Your Self Up (CYSU) content was new to me. I'm in my early 30s and this was the first time I'd been exposed to this type of self-awareness/mindfulness work. It has been beyond beneficial for me.

I've enjoyed learning to pay attention to myself and self-examining my reactions to things. It's been great to see that I am able to make a change—I can react differently right now in this moment.

The biggest takeaway for me from CYSU was the idea of stories. I have a mind that tends to run wild and conjure up all sorts of ideas about what might happen in a given situation. And then I would *accidentally* decide which one seemed most likely and then act as if that were *real*.

Just becoming aware of the fact that I'm always generating stories, and that it's natural because I'm human, was huge for me. It was astonishing to me to see this in this new light. I've shared this idea about stories with my wife, my mother, my friends and many others.

So, look, I can still get caught up in story. But whereas before I wasn't even aware that was happening, I now become aware of it. Sometimes right away, sometimes it may take some time. And when I become aware of it I remind myself I can take action instead of basking in the stress.

This literally happens *all the time* for me and I can say that becoming aware of this notion of stories has been transformative for me.

...becoming aware of this notion of stories has been **transformative** for me.

N. Patel, Commercial Real Estate & Private Financing Lending Broker

At a high level, the program helped me to become more mindful of my actions and how they impact the perceptions of the people around me (e.g., colleagues, customers, family members, etc.).

I identified a self-limiting behavior (SLB) where I frequently internalized other people's problems. As I paid more attention to that SLB, I realized I was afraid that if I did not exhibit this behavior, others would judge me and see me as "not caring." I also realized I was spreading myself way too thin by being overly-engaged in other people's situations AND I also had personal and family priorities that were not being attended to. I began to experiment with creating boundaries and stepping back a bit from other people's problems.

Here's a recent example. I have a close friend who is going through a difficult situation. I'm not "there for her" as much as I would have been in the past. Even just saying that can be hard for me. And yet I'm comfortable that I am there "enough."

And by better managing my boundaries and not getting sucked into her situation, I'm able to focus my energies on myself and on my nuclear family. I've got much less stress in my life and, almost counterintuitively, by creating more distance between me and my friend's problems, I'm more effective in helping her when she really needs me.

I took the CYSU program two-and-a-half years ago. While it hasn't been easy, and I still have room for improvement, I know I am continuing to do a much better job of managing my boundaries than I had been.

Ana Pease, HR Director

The Coach Your Self Up (CYSU) program helped me confirm a few self-limiting behaviors (SLBs) that I knew I wanted to work on but didn't know how to address—I didn't even know how to *start* to address them. I knew these SLBs were "holding me back" and knew that it would help me if I were able to make some changes.

CYSU showed me that there is a path to changing an SLB. The program gave me a set of tools to use, a set of techniques to try. I began making progress during the program itself.

I'm continually working on making small shifts. The shifts I have made in my behaviors are having a tangible positive impact on my relationships and my overall success.

As an HR leader, I have also introduced the concept of SLBs to many of the managers I work with. Educating managers on this concept often gives them more confidence to discuss SLB-related concerns directly with employees in a tactful and supportive way.

The other idea from this program that I have found to be very valuable is that of stories. This has been powerful in helping me be more aware of when I'm treating my stories as facts.

It's been really helpful to bring this concept in to coaching and mentoring discussions with colleagues and friends. It is a relatively simple concept that others can easily grasp. It can be quite eye-opening to others when they have that moment of realization that they are treating an assumption as a fact—and how big of an obstacle they've put in their own path by doing so.

It can be quite eye-opening to others when they have that moment of realization that they are treating an assumption as a fact— and **how big of an obstacle they've put in their own path** by doing so.

Leigh Faber, Operations Manager

For me there was a great awakening around the concept of stories. Realizing that not all of us have the same experience when sitting in a room together was a real eye-opener. This has led me to more frequently ask others about their perspectives pertaining to a shared experience.

This program helped me to see when I was making judgments and assumptions about others and situations. I was able to see that I was creating stories. I believe I've made a nice behavioral shift in this arena. I can now recognize when I am creating and projecting my stories (of course this is ongoing work!), of when stories are at play, and being curious to understand other people's perspectives.

I've learned to slow down and take a step back. I'm "looking inward" and assessing my reactions to people/situations. I'm paying more attention to how others are responding to me.

The techniques I learned in this program have also helped me bounce back from a difficult life situation. Using the attention management skills to bring myself back to the present moment has alleviated a lot of unnecessary stress from over-wallowing in unpleasant thoughts.

I'm "looking inward" and **assessing my reactions** to people/situations. I'm paying more attention to how *others* are responding to *me.*

Charles S., Sales Operations

First of all, I applaud my employer for offering this type of program. It sent a strong signal that they are interested in supporting my own personal growth and development.

During the program I worked on a self-limiting behavior I had of "not being open to input from others on my projects." I've gotten so much better at including others now.

Coach Your Self Up (CYSU) helped me work through the underlying reasons why I needed to be in control. And while I've still got a way to go on this particular behavior, I've definitely moved the needle and am more collaborative than I used to be.

One general thing from CYSU that has helped me both professionally and personally is learning to question my assumptions and perceptions. I realized I was often quick to jump to conclusions and that maybe my perceptions were not reality.

I now ask myself to check my assumptions. "What if another person has a different perspective?" And this is often the case.

One other positive fallout from my CYSU experience is that I started doing yoga. I want to be more mindful and find that yoga helps me to "get out of my head and into my body." Being more present is a good thing. I find it therapeutic. And I can confidently say this will take me the rest of my life.

It's been two years since I took the CYSU program and I am happy to say that it is, "A gift that keeps on giving."

Shafiq Taymuree, Executive Vice President

It was very insightful for me to consider my self-limiting behaviors. Not only that, but to start to dig underneath them and see where I had stories that were also self-limiting.

I realized I was creating artificial boundaries for myself. And when I was able to take down those boundaries, **new worlds opened up**.

Around the time I was taking the program, I was attending several networking events pertaining to my field/industry. I tended to hold back from much active participation.

As I examined this behavior, I realized that I had made up some stories about how the other people at these events were judging me. I was essentially judging myself through their eyes. I realized I was operating as if these people didn't want me there—which was just a story I had made up. I began to challenge those stories. How would I experiment with acting differently if I didn't believe those stories to be true?

Another tenet of the program that has helped me a lot is the idea of "small shifts lead to big changes." I don't need to make huge one-time changes. With one of these industry groups, I started becoming more participative in meetings. And now (over a year later), I'm a contributing member on a key committee and am in the process of running for a spot on the board.

This program opened me up to the world of self-work. Since the program I've engaged in numerous additional personal growth trainings and activities. I'm continuing to make strides toward "just being myself," which is really great.

Denise H., Acquisitions and Client Relations Manager

For me it all started with identifying my self-limiting behavior (SLB) of not being able to say "no" when people asked me to do things for them. I was a "yes" person all the way. This was unhealthy. It caused me lots of stress and frustration.

It also negatively impacted my relationships, both inside and outside of work. I sometimes neglected people I cared about because I was busy doing the things I said "yes" to. I often became resentful of the people who I said "yes" to.

It was a big deal for me **just to see that this was an SLB** that I could try to change.

As I paid more attention to my SLB, I found an underlying story. I believed that if I didn't say "yes," then I was a "bad" co-worker, a "bad" friend, a "bad" wife. I believed I would be viewed as unsupportive and therefore be loved/liked less by the other person. I was afraid to change this behavior because this story felt so strong and true for me.

Becoming more receptive to the notion that this was a story and not a fact opened me up to trying to make a change.

I found that as I've started to say "yes" less often, people don't ask me to do things for them as much as they used to. My experience is that many of these people are becoming more self-sufficient and taking more ownership themselves. This is helping them to grow both personally and professionally.

I still have some people-pleaser in me. However, I say "no" more frequently and my stress levels are much more manageable now.

Fernando Rosell, QA Engineer

I took the CYSU program about two-and-a-half years ago. I must say that I was a little skeptical about this type of program when I joined. Today, I remember it almost every day, as the theories we learned during the program apply to many aspects of my daily life.

What I learned during the CYSU program applies to basic activities of my life as well as to more important ones. It applies to my professional career as well as to my personal and family life.

There are some specific ideas and techniques from the program that I remember clearly:

- The concept that making a small change now can make a big difference in the future. This was encouraging.
- Challenging your stories. This helped me differentiate when something was a "fact" vs. an assumption or a story made up by me. I still make up these "stories," but the program helped me to be aware of when I'm doing so and gave me some tools to ensure that they don't "get in my way."
- Self-awareness and contemplation. It helped me realize how difficult it is nowadays to focus on a single task and to be in the moment. I now use some of the activities I like the most, such as hiking, biking and swimming as opportunities to work on being more present.

I'm glad I was able to join the classroom training program back then when it was offered by my employer. And I'm happy that now I can share the program as a book with my friends and family.

Chris R., Inside Sales Account Executive

Coach Your Self Up (CYSU) was one of the most insightful training programs I've had in my career. It gave me time for reflection and helped me realize that I was ready to do things differently.

The self-limiting behavior that I worked on during the program was to manage my temper more effectively. I knew that I had a tendency to get "hot-headed" at times and this program helped me to see how that might get in my way. CYSU gave me the tools to become much more self-aware of this behavior.

It helped me to identify the triggers, for example the hairs standing up on the back of my neck, that preceded this behavior. Whereas before I wasn't even aware of this, I was now learning to not only see my triggers but to use those signals to help me choose a different way of handling the situation. I am much calmer now than I used to be and this is noticeable not only to me but to others around me.

Another tool that I learned in this program was the Johari Window. This helps us think about how we perceive ourselves vs. how others perceive us. This tool has proven to be valuable to me in having career discussions with leaders that I trust to help me identify blind spots where I have additional opportunities to improve.

C. Johnson, Outside Field Representative/Consultant

The Coach Your Self Up (CYSU) program helped me become more self-aware. I'm much more conscious now of how my decisions impact others. I'm more thoughtful when making decisions in that I'm thinking through the impact on others in advance.

I'm a very self-critical person and this program helped me to not be so hard on myself. As I've learned to care more about myself, I find I'm also caring more about others. I'm much more empathetic than I used to be.

The self-limiting behavior that I worked on was that I had a tendency to talk over people—I was not a very good listener. I'm a better listener now. I fall back at times, but I become aware of it pretty quickly and am able to switch gears. I know how important it is to be a good listener.

This is big for me! Listening is a way to show others that you care. I used to be more defensive and quick with my rebuttals. Now I'm interested in staying curious. I really want to understand where the other person is coming from.

In many respects, there is an "old" me and a "new" me. I prefer the way the "new" me handles things.

Overall, CYSU was a catalyst that has helped me become much more conscious of what I am doing with my life. This program has helped me become a better person.

I'm a very self-critical person and this program helped me to **not be so hard on myself**. As I've learned to care more about myself, I find I'm also caring more about others. **I'm much more empathetic than I used to be**.

Appendix B
Organizational Application

This book is based upon the Coach Your Self Up (CYSU) training program that I created for use within organizations. In this appendix I highlight a few key challenges that CYSU can help an organization to address.

Career Development

As noted at the beginning of this book, I believe that personal development *is* career development. (If you are looking at this topic through an organizational lens, I encourage you to revisit the section "Personal Development *is* Career Development" on pages 1-2 for additional context.)

Employee engagement surveys often show that employees want their employers to be doing more for them in terms of supporting their career development. At the same time, employers are looking for employees to take more ownership of their own professional and personal development.

CYSU helps an organization to address both of those challenges. As also noted in Chapter 1, CYSU gives participants tools to "bend their future" by driving positive behavioral shifts. It is common for more opportunities to be presented to individuals who are demonstrating this level of self-initiative.

In my experience, workers in the "millennial" generation are much more interested in learning about themselves than my generation was at a similar relatively young age. I have found millennials are attracted to self-coaching and the exploration to become more self-aware, and to apply that to their growth and development.

Giving employees the chance—and the support—to better understand and address their blind spots, self-limiting beliefs or stories, **may be the most important step that today's leading organizations can take** to help individuals take ownership of and shape their career trajectories.

Here is a quote from Rich Jacquet, the Chief Human Resources Officer at a company that made CYSU part of their career development offerings:

> "What could be more helpful to employees for taking ownership of their careers than learning to see where their behaviors are getting in their way and giving them tools to address that?"

I believe self-coaching will be a cornerstone of the next generation of career development and employee engagement practices.

Coaching as Part of an Organization's Culture

As an executive coach and leadership trainer, I pay attention to the state of coaching within organizations. I have also spoken to several HR and Learning & Development leaders on this topic as research for this book.

Many leading organizations recognize the value of coaching. They invest in pairing leadership coaches with their senior leaders. Based on the success at the "top of the house," more organizations are utilizing coaches further down the org chart (i.e., investing in coaches to work with VP and Director level employees).

I have also found many organizations desire or expect that their leaders and managers will coach their employees. To that end, those organizations typically train all leaders (which includes all people managers) to coach their people. This is great. In practice, however, not all managers are created equal and some are more likely than others to embrace and/or be good at coaching.

Those organizations that are most active with promoting internal coaching practices are either implicitly or explicitly trying to build a "coaching culture." In addition to the items described above, you would be more likely to find internal coaches on staff at a company that is explicitly building a coaching culture.

My observation is that at most organizations that are building a coaching culture, all of the investment goes toward the leaders of the organization (e.g., providing them with professional training and coaching). To their credit, some of the leading organizations in this arena provide training to all their employees on "how to be coached."

In the last several years, the idea of "scalable coaching" has become a hot discussion topic within organizations that embrace a coaching culture. The intent is to find an affordable way to make coaching available to more people, most frequently front-line managers and high-potential individual contributors.

Numerous companies are addressing the challenge of scalable coaching. Skyline Group has a solution. Sidekick has a solution.

Careerwave has a solution. BetterManager has a solution. BetterUp has a solution. (I am sure there are many other companies offering solutions in this space and more will continue to emerge.)

All of these solutions involve interesting approaches for allowing individuals to interact directly with a coach. And I applaud all of these companies (and the others that are emerging) and wish them great success. More coaching for more people is a great thing.

While these approaches significantly reduce the cost of engaging coaches, it will continue to be difficult for most organizations to provide direct coaching to everyone.

Self-coaching can be a game-changer in the coaching culture arena. It is a new arrow an organization can put in its quiver. For relatively low levels of investment, employees can learn self-coaching skills that will help them to be better coachees, to be more adept at managing their attention and at driving their own behavior change—all while increasing their self-awareness.

Shifting to a more Mindful / Self-Aware / "Conscious" Culture

There are numerous ideas and movements afoot that place heightened emphasis on the value of having employees who are more mindful, self-aware, and "conscious." (In this context, the notion of "conscious" equates to higher levels of self-awareness. Just because somebody is breathing and showing up to work does not mean that they are "conscious"—there is more to it.)

Here is a list of various ideas and movements in this arena (in no particular order) that I am aware of:

- Conscious Capitalism
- Conscious Business
- Benefit Corporations
- B Corps
- Social Venture Network
- Wisdom 2.0
- Deliberately Developmental Organizations
- The Transformative Workplace
- Triple Bottom Line
- Self-Managing Organizations

For organizations that embrace one or more of these ideas, the notion of self-coaching is highly aligned with their underlying tenets pertaining to employees.

Jon Freeman, President of Stonecrest Financial, who was interested in helping his employees become more self-aware, said:

> "We ran most of our employees through Coach Your Self Up to expose them to what I believe are the gifts of self-awareness and taking ownership of their personal growth. While I can't put a dollar figure on it, this program delivered the results I was hoping for and I've seen a palpable positive change in our workplace. I'm excited to see our employees opening up more, engaging more, and being more empathic towards each other."

Leaders at All Levels

I have seen more and more organizations embracing this philosophy. In these organizations, a common message to employees is that you do not need to be in a leadership role to be a leader: "You are all leaders."

Bring Your Whole Self to Work

This is another mantra I have heard more organizations espousing of late. The idea is that people tend to have a work persona that differs from who they are outside the workplace. In organizations that want employees to "bring their whole selves to work," employees are encouraged to shed that work persona.

Individuals may try to hide their self-limiting behaviors, certainly their self-limiting beliefs (stories), at work. Coach Your Self Up can help these organizations help their employees to identify these aspects of themselves and to make it feel safe within the workplace for them to be working on these dimensions of personal growth.

Ongoing Feedback / Feedback Culture

There has been a significant shift taking place over the last several years with organizations moving away from annual performance ratings and reviews. In their place, these organizations are encouraging more frequent, ongoing feedback and development discussions between managers and their employees.

When employees are exposed to more frequent feedback on areas where they need to shift/improve their behavior, Coach Your Self Up provides a toolkit that employees can utilize to *act* on that ongoing feedback.

In all of these environments, organizations would benefit if employees were equipped for **effective self-leadership and self-management**. Coach Your Self Up can certainly help in this regard.

Coach Your Self Up in Your Organization

One or more of the topics described in this chapter may apply to your organization. Or perhaps you just loved the book and think it would be great if your employer offered this to employees.

If you think that your organization would benefit from offering Coach Your Self Up "in-house," I encourage you to bring this to the attention of the person in your organization who is responsible for employee development. This person often resides in the Human Resources department.

In addition to showing them this book, you could also point them to information about the eLearning version of this program at: coachyourselfup.com/course/paperback

You can contact me through my website at coachyourselfup.com or email me directly at mike@coachyourselfup.com.

Resources

I recommend the following resources, in no particular order, if you are interested in doing a deeper dive on any of these topics.

Self-Coaching

Online:

- Coach Your Self Up eLearning Program – coachyourselfup.com/course/paperback
- The Art of Self-Coaching (Stanford GSB course archive) edbatista.com/the-art-of-self-coaching-course.html

Books:

- *Self Coaching 101,* by Brooke Castillo
- *Get Unstuck & Get Going* by Michael Bungay Stanier
- *Drop It: A Coach's Secret to Productivity, Presence, and Possibility,* by Linda Newlin Ruffin
- *Self as Coach, Self as Leader,* by Pamela McLean

Attention / Self-awareness / Meditation

Online:

- Juniper – meditation tradition for modern life juniperpath.org
- Headspace – online meditation resources headspace.com
- Evenflow – online meditation resources evenflow.io
- Mechanics of Awakening – audio library exploring attention mechanicsofawakening.com/free-downloads.html

Attention / Self-awareness / Meditation (continued)

Books:

- *Search Inside Yourself: The Unexpected Path to Achieving Success, Happiness (and World Peace)*, by Chade-Meng Tan
- *Insight: The Surprising Truth About How Others See Us, How We See Ourselves, and Why the Answers Matter More Than We Think*, by Tasha Eurich
- *The Practice of Self-Management: A Handbook for Walking the Path from Reactivity to Presence and Connection*, by Christopher Forman and Bryan Ungard
- *Perceptual Integration: The Mechanics of Awakening*, by Gary Sherman
- *The Power of Now: A Guide to Spiritual Enlightenment*, by Eckhart Tolle
- *The Miracle of Mindfulness: An Introduction to the Practice of Meditation*, by Thich Nhat Hanh
- *Emotional Intelligence: Why it can Matter More Than IQ*, by Daniel Goleman
- *Emotional Intelligence 2.0*, by Travis Bradberry and Jean Greaves
- *Focus – The Hidden Driver of Excellence*, by Daniel Goleman

Neuroplasticity / Neuroscience

Online:

- BrainHQ – online brain exercises <u>brainhq.com</u>

Books:

- *My Stroke of Insight: A Brain Scientist's Personal Journey*, by Jill Bolte Taylor, Ph.D.
- *Buddha's Brain: The Practical Neuroscience of Happiness, Love, and Wisdom*, by Rick Hanson, Ph.D.
- *The Brain That Changes Itself: Stories of Personal Triumph from the Frontiers of Brain Science*, by Norman Doidge, M.D.
- *Soft-Wired: How the New Science of Brain Plasticity Can Change Your Life*, by Dr. Michael Merzenich, Ph.D.

Neuroplasticity / Neuroscience (continued)

- *Your Brain at Work: Strategies for Overcoming Distraction, Regaining Focus, and Working Smarter All Day Long,* by David Rock

Investigating Potential Deep Stories – The Enneagram & Positive Intelligence

Online:
- The Enneagram Institute enneagraminstitute.com
  Includes:
    o Online assessment, content, workshops
- Positive Intelligence positiveintelligence.com
  Includes:
    o Online "saboteur" assessment, TEDx video

Books:
- *The Wisdom of The Enneagram: The Complete Guide to Psychological and Spiritual Growth for the Nine Personality Types,* by Don Richard Riso and Russ Hudson
- *The Essential Enneagram: The Definitive Personality Test and Self-Discovery Guide,* by David Daniels, M.D. and Virginia Price, Ph.D.
- *The Complete Enneagram: 27 Paths to Greater Self-Knowledge,* by Beatrice Chestnut, Ph.D.
- *The Enneagram: Understanding Yourself and Others in Your Life,* by Helen Palmer
- *Positive Intelligence: Why Only 20% of Teams and Individuals Achieve Their True Potential and How You Can Achieve Yours,* by Shirzad Chamine

Career Development

Books:
- *Rebooting Work: Transform How You Work in the Age of Entrepreneurship,* by Maynard Webb

Career Development (continued)

- *Up is Not the Only Way: Rethinking Career Mobility*, by Beverley Kaye, Lindy Williams, and Lynn Cowart
- *The Start-up of You: Adapt to the Future, Invest in Yourself, and Transform Your Career*, by Reid Hoffman and Ben Casnocha

General Self-Care / Personal Growth

Online:

- Brené Brown's TED Talk "The Power of Vulnerability" www.ted.com/talks/brene_brown_on_vulnerability
- Amy Cuddy's Ted Talk "Your Body Language Shapes Who You Are" www.ted.com/talks/amy_cuddy_your_body_language_shapes_who_you_are
- Jia Jiang's TED Talk "What I Learned from 100 Days of Rejection." www.ted.com/talks/jia_jiang_what_I_learned_from_100_days_of_rejection (Jia's personal story about breaking through his self-limiting behaviors/beliefs around rejection.)

Books:

- *Loving What Is: Four Questions That Can Change Your Life*, by Byron Katie
- *The Gifts of Imperfection: Let Go of Who You Think You're Supposed to Be and Embrace Who You Are*, by Brené Brown, Ph.D., LMSW
- *Daring Greatly: How the Courage to Be Vulnerable Transforms the Way We Live, Love, Parent, and Lead*, by Brené Brown, Ph.D., LMSW
- *Rising Strong: How the Ability to Reset Transforms the Way We Live, Love, Parent, and Lead*, by Brené Brown, Ph.D., LMSW
- *Bring Your Whole Self to Work: How Vulnerability Unlocks Creativity, Connection, and Performance* by Mike Robbins

General Self-Care / Personal Growth (continued)

- *Nothing Changes Until You Do: A Guide to Self-Compassion and Getting Out of Your Own Way,* by Mike Robbins
- *Positively Resilient: 5½ Secrets to Beat Stress, Overcome Obstacles, and Defeat Anxiety,* by Doug Hensch
- *Atomic Habits: An Easy and Proven Way to Build Good Habits and Break Bad Ones,* by James Clear

Organizational Emphasis

Books:

- *Conscious Capitalism: Liberating the Heroic Spirit of Business,* by John Mackey and Raj Sisodia
- *Conscious Business: How to Build Value Through Values,* by Fred Kofman
- *An Everyone Culture: Becoming a Deliberately Developmental Organization,* by Robert Kegan and Lisa Laskow Lahey
- *The 15 Commitments of Conscious Leadership: A New Paradigm for Sustainable Success,* by Jim Dethmer, Diana Chapman, and Kaley Warner Klemp
- *The Transformative Workplace: Growing People, Purpose, Prosperity, and Peace,* by Carole and David Schwinn
- *Reinventing Organizations: A Guide to Creating Organizations Inspired by the Next Stage of Human Consciousness,* by Frederic Laloux

ACKNOWLEDGEMENTS

There are so many people who supported me in untold ways during my journey that led to this book. Here are a few.

Linda Newlin was my book coach and guided me on the development of this book since its inception. Her unwavering optimism and enthusiasm were instrumental. Linda's experience as a self-published author also proved super helpful in navigating the world of self-publishing.

Alice Chaffee worked tirelessly on editing my manuscript. Her input was invaluable -- from grammatical edits (apparently, I am pretty weak with the subjunctive) to big-picture insights.

Jon Freeman, Rich Jacquet, and Ana Pease have been super supportive by offering the Coach Your Self Up training program in their respective organizations on an ongoing basis.

Stacey Manes and Maenna Glenn were both willing to take a chance on me and launched the very first pilot programs of Coach Your Self Up within their respective companies.

While he may not realize it, Lawrence Levy had a big impact on the contents of this book. He played an important role in helping me shape the final design of the Coach Your Self Up training program.

Thanks to The Tribe, a men's consciousness group based in Northern California. This special group provided huge support and guidance that helped me see my stories and think deeply about the self I aspired to be. A special thanks to Michael Lipson, a member of The Tribe, for his coaching wisdom.

Finally, I want to thank my girlfriend and life partner, Ellen Brook. She has been fully supportive of my efforts to bring Coach Your Self Up into being. Whether I needed space or a quick kick-in-the-behind, she provided it. Thank you for being there for me Ellen.

Made in the USA
Monee, IL
17 August 2020